Dear Jesus

A MEMOIR

by Kari L. Orloff

Trilogy Christian Publishers
A Wholly Owned Subsidiary of Trinity Broadcasting Network
2442 Michelle Drive
Tustin, CA 92780

10 9 8 7 6 5 4 3 2 1

Library of Congress Cataloging-in-Publication Data is available.

B-ISBN#: 978-1-64773-678-1

E-ISBN#: 978-1-64773-679-8

To the one who believed in God's purpose for my life before I did. Thank you for seeing me, believing in me, encouraging me, and loving me well. I love you, Elizabeth.

To the man who knows me and loves me unconditionally. You are my best friend. Thank you for remaining steady, faithful, and allowing me to dream with God as He fulfills the plans, He has for me. I love you, Brandon.

To the best part of me: Kristian, Jakob, Lukas, and Ella. For God knows the plans He has for you, to prosper you and not harm you, but to give you a hope and a future. I love you.

To the bravest woman I know. A woman who waited thirty years for God's restoration. A woman who walks with grace, integrity, compassion, and love. Thank you for listening to me process and dream. I love you, Mom.

To my sister. The one who has shared this life with me. The good, the bad and everything in between. I love you, Kelly.

To my sisters in Christ. You know who you are. The women who walked with me through the pain, the women who prayed with me, loved me, and encouraged me. To the ones who played the littlest part to the greatest. I love you.

INTRODUCTION

DARKNESS VERSUS LIGHT

A dark cloud hovered overhead. Before long darkness loomed on every side. A flicker of light was moving toward Dothan. Darkness viewed the light from a distance and the scheming began. Joseph was up against the battle of his life, but nothing could ever stop God's plan. No weapon formed against him would ever prosper. (Is. 54:17) He may have been betrayed, sold, falsely accused, and imprisoned, but nothing could thwart God's purpose for his life. Joseph was chosen, anointed, and highly favored by the Lord. Even prison in a foreign country could not hold him from living his destiny. At just the right time Joseph was seen.

The plan seemed good to Pharaoh and to all his officials. So, Pharaoh asked them, "Can we find anyone like this man, one in whom is the spirit of God?"

Then Pharaoh said to Joseph, "Since God has made all this known to you, there is no one so discerning and wise as you. You shall be in charge of my palace, and all my people are to submit to your orders. Only with respect to the throne will I be greater than you."

So, Pharaoh said to Joseph, "I hereby put you in charge of the whole land of Egypt." Then Pharaoh took his signet ring from his finger and put it on Joseph's finger. He dressed him in robes of fine linen and put a gold chain around his neck. He had him ride in a chariot as his second-in-command, and people shouted before him, "Make way!" Thus, he put him in charge of the whole land of Egypt.

Genesis 41:37–43

Our God is the God of redemption. Beautiful redemption. "And we know that in all things God works for the good of those who love him, who have been called according to his purpose" (Rom. 8:28). Joseph was called.

Joseph said to his brothers, "Come close to me." When they had done so, he said, "I am your brother Joseph, the one you sold into Egypt! And now, do not be distressed and do not be angry with yourselves for selling me here, because it was to save lives that God sent me ahead of you. For two years now there has been famine in the land, and for the next five years there will be no plowing and reaping. But God sent me ahead of you to preserve for you a remnant on earth and to save your lives by a great deliverance.

So then, it was not you who sent me here, but God.

Genesis 45:4–8

This battle. This battle of Joseph's life. It was not against his brothers. It was so much bigger than this.

For our struggle is not against flesh and blood, but against the rulers, against the authorities, against the powers of this dark world and against the spiritual forces of evil in the heavenly realms.

Ephesians 6:12

What the darkness did not know was that the life-light blazed out of the darkness; the darkness could not put it out (John 1:5 MSG).

A dark cloud hovered overhead. Before long darkness loomed on every side. A flicker of light sparkled throughout the house. All who entered in entered a battleground. Darkness versus light. This would be the fight of her life. A fight for truth, love, joy, peace, forbearance, kindness, goodness, faithfulness, gentleness, and self-control.

It was a hot summer day. A snake slithered in presenting himself as one and delivering a completely different person. And no wonder, for Satan himself masquerades as an angel of light. (2 Cor. 11:14) The door was opened to a web of lies and secrets. As the lies and secrets began to hit the light the abuse began. Thunderous blows of verbal abuse ricocheted off her breastplate and she was directly under espionage attack. As more truth emerged fear overcame her. Mysterious happenings snuck into a quiet life. But God.

She did not just start following the Lord. She had been walking for a while. Trained by the best. He had prepared her for battle. Every step of her life led her to this one place. This place where she was ready for the biggest battle of her life. She knew without a doubt what she had to do. She had to put on the armor of God. (Eph. 6:11)

Finally, be strong in the Lord and in his mighty power. Put on the full armor of God, so that you can take your stand against the devil's schemes. For our struggle is not against flesh and blood, but against the rulers, against the authorities, against the powers of this dark world and against the spiritual forces of evil in the heavenly realms. Therefore, put on the full armor of God, so that when the day of evil comes, you may be able to stand your ground, and after you have done everything, to stand. Stand firm then, with the belt of truth buckled around your waist, with the breastplate of righteousness in place, and with your feet fitted with the readiness that comes from the gospel of peace. In addition to all this, take up the shield of faith, with which you can extinguish all the flaming arrows of the evil one. Take the helmet of salvation and the sword of the Spirit, which is the word of God. And pray in the Spirit on all occasions with all kinds of prayers and requests. With this in mind, be alert and always keep on praying for all the Lord's people.

Ephesians 6:10–18

For the word of God is alive and active. Sharper than any double-edged sword, it penetrates even to dividing soul and spirit, joints, and marrow; it judges the thoughts and attitudes of the heart.

Hebrews 4:12

Our God is the God of redemption. Beautiful redemption. "And we know that in all things God works for the good of those who love him, who have been called according to his purpose" (Rom. 8:28). She was called. This battle. This battle of her life. It was not against this one snake. It was so much bigger than this.

TABLE OF CONTENTS

ONE

July 2016
Dear Jesus,

It is the summer of 2016 and I have everything a girl could want, but I am not satisfied. My life is full and blessed with a husband who loves me, a beautiful family, a new house and a breathtaking property, a lifestyle coveted by many and yet I have a deep longing and loneliness that is always with me. A thought is ever-present with me, Jesus, is there something more?

Jesus, I long for satisfaction that will put this restless soul at peace. If it is not found in loved ones, work, money, property, health, looks, success, or performance where can it be found? I have been seeking satisfaction as a hidden treasure with all my heart and soul only to find it was hidden inside of me the whole time.

I found You, Jesus, in the stillness of my day. As quietness entered my days and thankfulness left my lips, I saw you move and breathe and have Your being. You have taken my private prayers and decorated my views with glory only You can provide. When I make secret requests and You answer me, an awe takes root where the ache used to reside. Jesus, an awe is worth seeking, searching, questioning, and wrestling for. For when my ache is quenched, I am satisfied.

"Blessed are you who hunger now, for you will be satisfied" (Luke 6:21).

"As for me, I will be vindicated and will see your face; when I awake, I will be satisfied with seeing your likeness" (Ps. 17:15).

"I will be fully satisfied as with the richest of foods; with singing lips my mouth will praise you" (Ps. 63:5).

"Everyone's toil is for their mouth, yet their appetite is never satisfied" (Eccl. 6:7).

"After he has suffered, he will see the light of life and be satisfied; by his knowledge, my righteous servant will justify many, and he will bear their iniquities" (Isa. 53:1).

"SATISFIED"

Lonely
quiet
only thoughts
running through my mind
but then
there it was
HIM
a soft I love you
a sun-drop just opening
sun rays fall on perfect arms
window frames perfect moon
essential words on my screen
smell of fresh cut grass
tan arms passing by
colors splash across the hill
a moment
pulled in close perfect curve
rough hands
ten sparkling eyes looking at me
a fawn drinking from his mother
laughter
aching grins
wind blowing on my face
water crashing
full moon adjacent burnt orange sun
boat floating underneath
soft hand on my foot
wafer sharing
swimsuit shadows
bat ball cracking sound

a smile
smell of cherry wafting by
big black nose in my face
soft paw on my lap
fire crackles
guitar strums
small hands fire circling spinning
marshmallow dripping
a request for His word
breathless
heart swells
beauty everywhere
His LOVE
overwhelms
awestruck
tears spill
joy fulfilled
satisfied.

TWO

Dear Jesus,

My family treasure is situated neatly on the barn beam over head the burnt orange kitchen. As our life continues day-by-day, movement begins to shift the trinket. It is in the heat of the summer and belongings and personalities are sticky. School is just around the corner and Brandon is out of town. Jesus, my unexpected visit went awry, and I am finally able to breathe as I see the dust billow behind the truck leaving our long dirt drive. Life commenced until the vicious words entered my existence. These words were unwarranted, unwanted, and irrevocable. My family treasure slid off the edge of the barn beam and shattered. Shards of glass splattered across the dark pine wood. My life feels like this treasure. Broken. Life will never be the same.

"Be strong and courageous. Do not be afraid or terrified because of them, for the LORD your God goes with you; he will never leave you nor forsake you" (Deut. 31:6).

"The LORD is close to the brokenhearted and saves those who are crushed in spirit" (Ps. 34:18).

"BROKEN"

broken
shattered
many pieces on the ground
As the light hits
it glistens, shines
sharp and scattered
some a million miles away
picking up pieces one by one
some are obvious
others hidden
digging deep to find what lies beneath
this one beautiful
this one dull
inside
aching, raw
scarring, slicing
cutting deep
so many pieces on the ground
one by one
sifting through
holding, crying
letting go
this one keep
this one go
so many pieces on the ground

THREE

October 2016
Dear Jesus,

You are a mighty God. You are near. You are faithful. You hear me. I lay on the couch day after day and cry out to You. I know You hear me God. As I read Your word repeatedly you help me. I am hurting worse than I have ever hurt, God. I have lost someone incredibly special to me. I feel buried alive with grief and at the same time I am afraid. How can I go on? How long will this take? How will this end? I do not have any answers. I am so broken God. Thank You that You can restore me.

"I will repay you for the years the locusts have eaten—the great locust and the young locust, the other locusts and the locust swarm—my great army that I sent among you" (Joel 2:25).

"And the God of all grace, who called you to his eternal glory in Christ, after you have suffered a little while, will himself restore you and make you strong, firm, and steadfast" (1 Pet. 5:10).

"You intended to harm me, but God intended it for good to accomplish what is now being done, the saving of many lives" (Gen. 50:20).

"BEAUTIFUL REDEMPTION"

I stood at the foot of the mountain
few words
shocked, lost, broken
I looked up
steep
after the fire came a gentle whisper (1 Kings 19:12)
just breathe
I took one step
narrow road (Matt. 7:14)
another step
believe
step
for I know the plans I have for you (Jer. 29:11)
step
I will restore you (Joel 2:25)
step
you are essential
step
you are chosen (Jer. 1:4-8)
step
you are set apart (Jer. 1:4-8)
step
there are more with us than those who are with them (2 Kings 6:16)
step
I am doing something new
step
I am making a way in the wilderness (Isa. 43:16, 18–19)
step

you are a light
step
I will fight for you (Ex. 14:14)
step
do not be afraid (2 Kings 6:14)
step
I go before you (Deut. 31:8)
step
you are not alone (Isa. 43:2)
step
I will hear you when you call to me (Ps. 5:3)
step
I will do immeasurably more than you ask or imagine (Eph. 3:20)
step
I hold your right hand (Isa. 41:13)
step
I am close to the brokenhearted and
save those who are crushed in spirit (Ps. 34:18)
step
it is I you must follow (Deut. 13:4)
step
I will teach you what to do (Ex. 4:15)
step
there is nothing too hard for me (Jer. 32:27)
step
the battle is not yours (2 Chr. 20:15)
step
even youths grow tired and weary (Isa. 40:30)
step
I will strengthen and help you (Isa. 41:10b)
step
I have called you (Isa. 42:6)

step
when I act who can reverse it? (Isa. 43:13b)
step
my purpose will stand (Isa. 46:10)
step
I will teach you what is best for you and
direct you in the way you should go (Isa. 48:17)
step
I will never leave you (Heb. 13:5)
step
I am still on the mountain.
There is only one Voice leading me.

FOUR

October 2016
Dear Jesus,

I feel like I have spent years in the desert walking. Aimlessly walking. I was always seeking. Always searching. But I see now it was aimless still. Jesus, this ultimate betrayal has left me immobile. I cannot even walk aimlessly. I have been lying still. You see my tears flowing endlessly. Thank You for receiving my wordless prayers as I sit still in Your presence. I have poured over Your word for days, months even. In the stillness of my days, a clear directive emerged. Thank You for Your guidance. Now as I begin to move again, it is sure and steady and clear. The path for my feet is secure on Your narrow road. There is no more guessing. No more aimless walking. I will praise You.

You are providing me with sure footing, but not only this. You are providing me with the hope I need to keep moving forward. I do not want to be stuck in my pain spinning my tires, spraying mud. I want traction, mobility. I want my life to commence. Your bold, powerful voice is giving me courage to move and believe there is something worth fighting for. Each day now as I get up and begin moving forward, I eagerly seek You on the narrow road. I have a deep anticipation the prize is worth fighting for.

> Enter through the narrow gate. For wide is the gate and broad is the road that leads to destruction, and many enter through it. But small is the gate and narrow the road that leads to life, and only a few find it.
>
> Matthew 7:13–14

"For this God is our God for ever and ever; he will be our guide even to the end" (Ps. 48:14)

"In the beginning was the Word, and the Word was with God, and the Word was God" (John 1:1).

> In the same way, the Spirit helps us in our weakness. We do not know what we ought to pray for, but the Spirit himself intercedes for us through wordless groans. And he who searches our hearts knows the mind of the Spirit, because the Spirit intercedes for God's people in accordance with the will of God.
>
> Romans 8:26–27

"I press on toward the goal to win the prize for which God has called me heavenward in Christ Jesus" (Phil. 3:14).

FIVE

October 26, 2016
Dear Jesus,

The realization crept in as the morning light slinked past the curtains. The dust settled and I know the truth. I have no control. I cannot make others love me, choose me, or even like me. I cannot make others behave a certain way. I cannot make people see what I see, know what I know. I cannot make what is important to me important to others. I cannot make loved ones surrender. I cannot make lies truth. I cannot make hurtful words disappear. I cannot make sin go away. I cannot heal broken hearts. No matter how hard I try and no matter what avenue I take, I cannot do it.

For me this is the beginning of all wisdom. As I let go, Jesus, I hear You gently whisper, *I will.* Something beautiful is beginning to happen as I let go. As I transfer my burden to You, Jesus, its rightful owner, I begin to feel free. Thank You that Your plan and Your purpose will always stand.

"Many are the plans in a person's heart, but it is the LORD's purpose that prevails" (Prov. 19:21).

"Our God is in heaven; he does whatever pleases him" (Ps. 115:3).

So that from the rising of the sun to the place of its setting people may know there is none besides me. I am the LORD, and there is no other. I form the light and create darkness, I bring prosperity and create disaster; I, the LORD, do all these things.
Isaiah 45:6–7

"The LORD Almighty has sworn, 'Surely, as I have planned, so it will be, and as I have purposed, so it will happen'" (Is. 14:24).

"In his hand is the life of every creature and the breath of all mankind" (Job 12:10).

> Yours, LORD, is the greatness and the power and the glory and the majesty and the splendor, for everything in heaven and earth is yours. Yours, LORD, is the kingdom; you are exalted as head over-all. Wealth and honor come from you; you are the ruler of all things. In your hands are strength and power to exalt and give strength to all.
>
> 1 Chronicles 29:11–12

"The fear of the LORD is the beginning of wisdom, and knowledge of the Holy One is understanding" (Proverbs 9:10).

"I WILL"

I will pour water on the thirsty ground. (Isa. 44:3)
I will pour out my spirit on your offspring. (Isa. 44:3)
I will not forget you. (Isa. 44:21)
I will restore. (Isa. 44:26)
I will go before you. (Isa. 45:2)
I will break down gates of bronze and
cut through bars of iron. (Isa. 45:2)
I will give you the treasures of darkness,
riches stored in secret places. (Isa. 45:3)
I will strengthen you. (Isa. 45:5)
I will carry you. (Isa. 46:4)
I will sustain you. (Isa. 46:4)
I will rescue you. (Isa. 46:4)
I will do all I please. (Isa. 46:10)
I will grant salvation. (Isa. 46:13)
I will tell you of new things. (Isa. 48:6)
I will make you a light. (Isa. 49:6)
I will answer you. (Isa. 49:8)
I will help you. (Isa. 49:8)
I will keep you. (Isa. 49:8)
I will save. (Isa. 49.25)

SIX

October 26, 2016
Dear Jesus,

I am exhausted today, but Brandon seems to have as much energy as the kids. Every night is a routine. It is not regimented, but the evening usually ends in this way. Brandon, watching, *Leave it to Beaver or Rocky* with the boys wrestling on their bedroom floor. I usually tuck Ella into bed and sing "Jesus Loves Me." I always pause leaving room for her little voice to chime in, "Yes, Jesus loves me." My heart just swells hearing her sing these sweet words. But always after we sing, I turn on her *Frozen* night light and push the button on her purple ladybug pillow pet which streams soft, pale light on her ceiling. I love how the light in her room dispels the darkness. There is just something about darkness, Jesus, that is unsettling. Jesus, Your word says that in darkness lie hidden things, captives, and fear. Darkness is debilitating and crippling. I know there is something more to this life. There is something healing, cleansing, and liberating. It is Your light, Lord. Your light pierces through the darkness and cuts straight to the core. It breaks every boundary, illuminating and revealing deep and hidden things. Your light is freeing and truth seeking. In Your light, I can see. Plainly.

I love light. I love the light of a campfire crackling in the dark night air. I love the light of Christmas illuminating trees and houses. Streets and lamp posts. I love the light from the stars sparkling brilliantly against the black night sky. I love the light of a flashlight revealing a narrow path. I love the light of a candle flickering in a dark room. I love sun rays piercing through the clouds. I love the sun setting, casting orange, pink, and purple. Light ignites. It is brilliant

29

and radiant. It glistens and shines to the depths. Light exposes and remains beautiful and alive. Hopeful. You are calling me to come into the Light. I stand and gaze upon Your beauty.

Jesus, I hear You. I am taking a chance and stepping into the light. I am coming completely clean and exposing all my insecurity, shame, and brokenness. I am sitting with You Jesus and allowing You to begin Your work in my life. I love just sitting with You, Jesus. I am baring my soul in Your presence. Thank You for infusing Your light and healing me from the inside out. Today I am choosing to bask in the One who sees plainly. You Jesus.

> "But whoever lives by the truth comes into the light, so that it may be seen plainly that what they have done has been done in the sight of God" (John 3:21).

> "When Jesus spoke again to the people, he said, 'I am the light of the world. Whoever follows me will never walk in darkness but will have the light of life'" (John 8:12).

> "For it is God who works in you to will and to act in order to fulfill his good purpose" (Phil. 2:13).

> "For we are God's handiwork, created in Christ Jesus to do good works, which God prepared in advance for us to do" (Eph. 2:10).

> "The light shines in the darkness, and the darkness has not overcome it" (John 1:5).

> "He reveals deep and hidden things; he knows what lies in darkness, and light dwells with him" (Dan. 2:22).

SEVEN

October 31, 2016
Dear Jesus,

Until I stepped into Your light, I had no idea who I was. I did not know to whom I belonged or where I was going. I did not know the truth from a lie. I have lived my entire life paralyzed by the chaos in my mind. Loud, swirling thoughts running through my brain. Someone said something about me recently that is so harsh, cruel, and untrue. It did not just happen one time. It is happening repeatedly. These thoughts and comments are so loud they rule my consciousness. They take over. All. Of. Me.

It all began to make sense when I treaded through the pages of my worn childhood Bible. There is a war in my mind because I am in a constant battle. I read in Eph. 6:12, for our struggle is not against flesh and blood, but against the rulers, against the authorities, against the powers of this dark world and against the spiritual forces of evil in the heavenly realms. I learned I have an adversary who wants nothing more than to disrupt my peace. This adversary is a great enemy of my soul who wants nothing more than to create division, chaos, and doubt in my life. He is an accuser who thrives in telling lies that I believe! I do not want to believe these lies anymore.

Your truth is beginning to take root and the battle in my mind is beginning to make sense. As I begin to wage war with Your word the lies are beginning to lose their grip on me. I began to read Ephesians 1 and 2 and I learned the truth about myself. I am blessed. I am chosen. I am loved. I am a child of God. I am wanted. I am forgiven. I am joined to Christ. I am saved. I am sealed. I am free. I am a new creation created to fulfill the plans You have for me. I used to be hopeless and now I am hope-filled. I used to be far from You, God, and now I am close. Day by day I am learning to take every thought captive to make it obedient to You because Your word is the ultimate truth. It is sharper than any two-edged sword cutting straight to the thoughts and intentions of the heart. Every thought of mine needs to be washed by Your word so that I can know the truth from the lie. Who said these words? Are they true? The only way for me to know for sure is to know Your word. As I begin slowing down, reading my Bible, and sitting with You, Jesus, the loud, swirling thoughts begin to diminish. The truth is becoming greater than the lies. I am throwing out the lies, doubt and shame and I am being made new in the attitude of my mind.

> Do not conform to the pattern of this world but be transformed by the renewing of your mind. Then you will be able to test and approve what God's will is—his good, pleasing, and perfect will.
> Romans 12:2

"We demolish arguments and every pretension that sets itself up against the knowledge of God, and we take captive every thought to make it obedient to Christ" (2 Cor. 10:5).

> For our struggle is not against flesh and blood, but against the rulers, against the authorities, against the powers of this dark world and against the spiritual forces of evil in the heavenly realms.
> Ephesians 6:12

> Then I heard a loud voice in heaven say: "Now have come the salvation and the power and the kingdom of our God, and the authority of his Messiah. For the accuser of our brothers and sisters, who accuses them before our God day and night, has been hurled down.
> Revelation 12:10

You belong to your father, the devil, and you want to carry out your father's desires. He was a murderer from the beginning, not holding to the truth, for there is no truth in him. When he lies, he speaks his native language, for he is a liar and the father of lies.

John 8:44

"For the word of God is alive and active. Sharper than any double-edged sword, it penetrates even to dividing soul and spirit, joints, and marrow; it judges the thoughts and attitudes of the heart" (Heb. 4:12).

"Sanctify them by the truth; your word is truth" (John 17:17).

"Greater is He who is in you than he who is in the world" (1 John 4:4).

"But whoever is united with the Lord is one with him in spirit" (1 Cor. 6:17).

"So, God created mankind in his own image, in the image of God he created them; male and female he created them" (Gen.1:27).

"Now you are the body of Christ, and each one of you is a part of it" (1 Cor. 12:27).

EIGHT

November 6, 2016
Dear Jesus,

I am feeling vulnerable. Exposed, if You will. Sharing my thoughts creates a lot of self-doubt. My mind is always in over-drive, so You will have to hang on. I am known to be called half-sentence by more than one person in my family. I have come to appreciate my brain is like a big 'ol plate of spaghetti; all interwoven and messy. I just have so many thoughts.

Well, today started with a beautiful verse from Your word. Back up a minute. It started with a feeling of discouragement. A feeling of tiredness and hopelessness. Wondering how will this trial end? Will I ever stop thinking about it? Dreaming about it? As usual I stepped out of my bed and wandered two steps to my window. I grabbed my phone and clicked on my email. Then, there it was, a beautiful verse from Your word. The verse said, "making known to us the mystery of his will, according to his purpose which he set forth in Christ as a plan for the fullness of time, to unite all things in him, things in heaven and things on earth" (Eph. 1:9–10) Unite! That is what You want, Jesus! Jesus, this gives me so much hope and encourages me. It tells me how this will end. You will unite all things in heaven and earth to Yourself.

You are the creator of the universe and with You all things hold together. There is no one like You. One day, at the name of Jesus every knee will bow. Power and majesty are Yours. When the times reach their fulfillment, You will bring all things together! I will praise Your holy name.

In this life, Jesus, it is so easy to be distracted and overwhelmed by my view. My life on earth is messy and flooded with brokenness.

35

It is in my home, my health, my finances, my relationships, and everything my hands touch, but one thing remains. I am not alone. For all are affected by the wages of sin. When I placed my trust in You, Jesus, as my Lord and Savior, I became Your child, an heir in the kingdom. As I walk with You and talk with You and follow Your ways, You promise to work all things together for my good because of my love for You. You have a plan and a purpose for my life, to give me a hope and a future. As I act justly, love mercy and humbly walk with You, You will give me peace. Here in this world I will have trouble, but You, Jesus, have overcome the world to set me free from sin and death.

This life is not about me. It is about You, sending Your son to redeem Your lost children. I live here in this world and all trials are a privilege for me because You are allowing me to take part in Your master plan to unite all things to Yourself so that one day, I will have eternal love, joy and peace with You and Your people. So, I will release my pain, my prayers, my hopes, and my desires to the palm of Your hands. I will praise You and trust You as You work all things for my good. I will stand for my house. I will stand for my husband, my marriage, and my children. I will stand for my health and the health of my loved ones. I will stand with You for my work and my finances. I will stand as I grieve. You are so faithful. You will never leave me or forsake me. You have a beautiful, marvelous plan to unite all things on heaven and earth to Yourself. I will forever praise You, Jesus.

"That at the name of Jesus every knee should bow, in heaven and on earth and under the earth, and every tongue acknowledge that Jesus Christ is Lord, to the glory of God the Father" (Phil. 2:10–11).

"No one is like you, LORD; you are great, and your name is mighty in power" (Jer. 10:6).

For in him all things were created: things in heaven and on earth, visible and invisible, whether thrones or powers or rulers

or authorities; all things have been created through him and for him. He is before all things, and in him all things hold together.
Colossians 1:16–17

"And we know that in all things God works for the good of those who love him, who have been called according to his purpose" (Rom. 8:28).

"For I know the plans I have for you," declares the LORD, "plans to prosper you and not to harm you, plans to give you hope and a future" (Jer. 29:11).

"I have told you these things, so that in me you may have peace. In this world you will have trouble. But take heart! I have overcome the world" (John 16:33).

"For the wages of sin is death, but the gift of God is eternal life in Christ Jesus our Lord" (Rom. 6:23).

"He has shown you, O mortal, what is good. And what does the LORD require of you? To act justly and to love mercy and to walk humbly with your God" (Micah 6:8).

"Be strong and courageous. Do not be afraid or terrified because of them, for the LORD your God goes with you; he will never leave you nor forsake you" (Deut. 31:6).

"Therefore, put on the full armor of God, so that when the day of evil comes, you may be able to stand your ground, and after you have done everything, to stand" (Eph. 6:13).

NINE

November 7, 2016
Dear Jesus,

I am feeling very vulnerable right now after reading and hearing terrible things someone wrote about me. I have always critiqued everything about myself and been unsatisfied with every detail of me. I have always felt like I am not enough. I am confused and I want to know what You say about me. I turned to Your word to find out what You think of me. It was just the words I needed to hear.

You think I am special. You made me fearfully and wonderfully. I am unique, one of a kind and known. Even my hairs on my head are numbered. You know everything about me, and You love me so much. I was created in Your image for good works that You prepared in advance for me to do. You have special plans for just me. I do not need to fit in. I was not created to be like everyone else. I have been set apart and chosen for something great. There is no one just like me.

You are the potter and I am the clay. Thank You for molding me, bending me, and shaping me according to Your purpose. Thank You for choosing me for Your own possession to bring praise to Your name. Help me press boldly into Your presence as You shine Your light down on me as I step into my calling. Thank You for my gifts, talents, and my ideas. I cannot conceive the things You have prepared for me. Thank You for always doing immeasurably more than I ask or imagine. You are a good, good Father.

"What no eye has seen, what no ear has heard, and what no human mind has conceived-the things God has prepared for those who love him" (1 Cor. 2:9).

39

For you created my inmost being, you knit me together in my mother's womb. I praise you because I am fearfully and wonderfully made; your works are wonderful; I know that full well. My frame was not hidden from you when I was made in the secret place, when I was woven together in the depths of the earth. Your eyes saw my unformed body; all the days ordained for me were written in your book before one of them came to be.

Psalm 139:13–16

"Indeed, the very hairs of your head are all numbered" (Luke 12:7).

"Each of you should use whatever gift you have received to serve others, as faithful stewards of God's grace in its various forms" (1 Pet. 4:10).

You know when I sit and when I rise; you perceive my thoughts from afar. You discern my going out and my lying down; you are familiar with all my ways. Before a word is on my tongue you, LORD, know it completely.

Psalm 139:2–4

"But you are a chosen race, a royal priesthood, a holy nation, a people for his own possession, that you may proclaim the excellencies of him who called you out of darkness into his marvelous light" (1 Pet. 2:9).

"Before I formed you in the womb, I knew you, and before you were born, I consecrated you; I appointed you a prophet to the nations" (Jer. 1:5).

"But now, O LORD, you are our Father; we are the clay, and you are our potter; we are all the work of your hand" (Isa. 64:8).

"But when he who had set me apart before I was born, and who called me by his grace" (Gal. 1:15).

"For now we see only a reflection as in a mirror; then we shall see face to face. Now I know in part; then I shall know fully, even as I am fully known" (1 Cor. 13:12).

"For just as each of us has one body with many members, and these members do not all have the same function" (Rom. 12:4).

"For we are God's handiwork, created in Christ Jesus to do good works, which God prepared in advance for us to do" (Eph. 2:10).

TEN

November 9, 2016
Dear Jesus,

Will my tears ever stop? I pour out my heart to You day after day. Salted tears touch my lips day in and day out. I am angry. I feel scared. At times I even feel hopeless.

I am recalling another time when I felt this way. At that time, I learned that sometimes I must give up and trust You. I thought back then that I could do something, find an answer, work through it, do anything to make things better, and I tried everything in my own strength. I learned at that critical time that You cannot rationalize with someone who is irrational. I truly learned what it meant to pray for my enemy. I learned at that time that You are my hope. My relationship with You was solidified at that time. It was where I learned to pray continually. It was when I learned how to surrender to Your will. It was when I learned to thank You through trials, and it was when I saw You the most intimately. I learned You are always near, and You hear me. I learned You are faithful. I learned to look for You and see You in my daily life. Whether it was a song at just the right time, a person's words or actions, a rainbow, or a beautiful sunset, I knew You were with me. I have seen You show up in the most unexpected places and I have seen You do so many miraculous things. You are always good, amazing, and faithful. I know that You have prepared me for where I am today. I will take the things that I have learned before and apply them to my heart today.

"I will hear you when you call to me" (Ps. 5:3).

"Those who cry as they plant their crops will sing with joy when they gather them in" (Ps. 126:5).

"Your kingdom come your will be done" (Matt. 6:10).

"The LORD himself goes before you and will be with you; he will never leave you nor forsake you. Do not be afraid; do not be discouraged" (Deut. 31:8).

"The horse is prepared for the day of battle, but victory belongs to the LORD" (Prov. 21:31).

"For we are His workmanship, created in Christ Jesus for good works, which God prepared beforehand so that we would walk in them" (Eph. 2:10)

"This is the word of the LORD to Zerubbabel: 'Not by might nor by power, but by my Spirit,' says the LORD Almighty" (Zech. 4:6).

"Pray continually" (1 Thess. 5:17).

"For you have been my hope, Sovereign LORD, my confidence since my youth" (Ps. 71:5).

"But I tell you, love your enemies and pray for those who persecute you" (Matt. 5:44).

ELEVEN

November 30, 2016

Dear Jesus,

Joy. Inexpressible joy. Where is it? I want it. Long for it. Need it. For so long I have been beaten down, broken, tired and wanting joy. Inexpressible joy. I want my funky back and a little bounce in my step. I long for a smile on my face. I want this and I want it to be real. Not just the fake happy, everything's great lie. The real deal. Joy.

I am beginning to pray before my feet hit the floor. Restore to me the joy of Your salvation. (Ps. 51:12) Before my kids even woke up today, I had a phone call. It was from a dear friend who loves me well. This woman has been praying for me and pouring into my life Your word. Today she just wanted me to know that she was praying for me and that she loved me. As I was preparing my kids for school today, I kept thinking about joy and how much I wanted to see it in my life. I kept praying over and over Your word. Restore to me the joy of Your salvation. (Ps. 51:12) As the kids hopped out of the van and the door closed, I decided I was going to spend time being thankful. I was going to count my blessings and get a new perspective. Jesus, as I sat down with You and read Your word a calmness swept over me.

When it was time for me to pick Ella up from school, I stopped quickly at the mailbox to get the mail. A gift I picked out for someone special for Christmas arrived. I was excited to see the finished product. The package was so pretty, stamped and decorated with the words written on it, "Open me already!" I sat at the end of my driveway and opened the package. I wanted to see what I designed come to life. Inside the package was a post card from the woman who made it. It read, "Today I am praying unending JOY over you. There is such goodness in your beautiful heart, and I pray you will know just how valued, loved, and cared for you are by Daddy God. Go be love, sister, cheering you on!"

Jesus, my jaw dropped. You are so good. I love how You meet me so personally, love me so well and extravagantly. You are a benevolent Father. I will tell of all Your wonderful deeds all the days of my life. (Ps. 105:2) When I told my good friend that called me this morning about this, she told me that the verse she was praying over me was that You would restore to me the joy of Your salvation. (Ps. 51:12) You are so near. You hear me and I love You. Thank You for activating a little joy in my heart today. I pray over all those who love me and all those I love. I pray they will know this real personal relationship with You, Jesus.

TWELVE

December 2, 2016
Dear Jesus,

I pray for unending joy today. I pray for peace in my heart. I pray I would see all You have in store for me today. I claim victory today in Your great name!

Three months ago, my life as I knew it changed. A big lie was exposed, and it is a lie that affects every part of my life from birth to today. Over the years I saw glimpses, but nothing could have prepared me for what I have learned and have been experiencing. I do not want to be going through this pain and this trial right now or ever for that matter. I want the verbal abuse and manipulation to stop. My mind and my health are feeling the effects. I do not want to engage in this dark world any longer. I refuse to stand with this lie. I have chosen to stand in the light. I have chosen to sever this hold at the root. I am willing to stand with You Jesus even if I am the only one standing.

Through previous struggles I learned to create boundaries for protection. I have decided to create a boundary now. It does not feel loving, but I know there is life and death in the power of the tongue. I know our struggle is not against flesh and blood and I know that the enemy comes to steal, kill, and destroy my life. You come to give me a full life and this boundary helps me secure the abundant life You offer.

Your words have authority and power. Your words are life and truth. I am choosing to speak life. I read Your word, I speak it out loud, I sing it, and drench my life with it. Thank You for Your word.

This afternoon I was singing the words, "Bless the Lord oh my soul, oh my soul, worship His holy name," and I felt peace wash over me. I continued singing and praising You as I left my driveway. As I was talking to You in the car, I rounded a corner and a beautiful

47

skyline appeared. It was cut in half with light at the bottom and a deep purple on the top. Piercing through, across my entire viewing capability, were holes of light. Brilliant light.

As I whispered, thanks to You, I heard the words, "Bless the Lord oh my soul, oh my soul, worship His holy name," play through my speakers. It was the most melodious sound. You know what? You take my breath away. As I was searching for my breath and my phone in the car, tears trickled down my cheeks. I fumbled with the phone as I tried to capture this gift You offered me. Today I chose life. I chose to put on my full armor. I had my helmet strapped on securely and all Your weapons at my disposal. I had the belt of truth fastened, the breastplate of righteousness in place, the shoes of the gospel of peace on, the shield of faith ready, the helmet of salvation secured and Your sword of the Spirit. My enemy did not stand a chance today. As I walked, relied on Your word, and applied You to my heart today I was left with life in the full. As I drew water from Your wells of salvation I was left with joy and peace. Thank You for the abundant life You offer. Thank You for Your protection and Your nearness. Thank You for Your joy and peace.

"With joy, you will draw water from the wells of salvation" (Isa. 12:3).

> For our struggle is not against flesh and blood, but against the rulers, against the authorities, against the powers of this dark world and against the spiritual forces of evil in the heavenly realms. Therefore, put on the full armor of God, so that when the day of evil comes, you may be able to stand your ground, and after you have done everything, to stand. Stand firm then, with the belt of truth buckled around your waist, with the breastplate of righteousness in place, and with your feet fitted with the readiness that comes from the gospel of peace. In addition to all this, take up the shield of faith, with which you can extinguish all the flaming arrows of the evil one. Take the helmet of salvation

and the sword of the Spirit, which is the word of God.

Eph. 6:12–17

"The thief comes only to steal and kill and destroy; I have come that they may have life and have it to the full" (John 10:10).

"The tongue has the power of life and death, and those who love it will eat its fruit" (Proverbs 18:21).

"Sanctify them by the truth; your word is truth" (John 17:17).

"Then Jesus came to them and said, 'All authority in heaven and on earth has been given to me'" (Matthew 28:18).

THIRTEEN

January 12, 2017
Dear Jesus,

The older I get the more trials I experience. I guess that makes sense. I was just thinking about how great You are the other day. Your ways are so high. I cannot understand them. How can I be experiencing so much searing pain and joy at the same time? Only with You, Jesus. The greater the trial I experience, the clearer I see You. I was just thinking about how You delivered me from my last trial when I saw a rainbow in the sky. I will never look at another rainbow the same again. Thank You for Your beauty and Your promises.

On January 21, 2013 I was driving in my van and praying and thanking You for blessing my family. I was smack in the middle of a season of suffering, but in the midst, I saw Your blessings. At that time, I was learning to thank You in the storm. I was getting ready to go on a trip and I was thanking You for allowing me to go on this trip and for the new pair of sandals I had just purchased. As I was praising You, I looked up and saw a rainbow cloud. Only You could bless me with a multi-colored cloud. I remember laughing out loud and thanking You for it. As I was looking at rainbow clouds and singing, "While I'm Waiting," by John Waller, I began to think about how You used the movie, *Fireproof*, and this song to teach me what love is. Your love. It is when I learned love is sacrificial. It is when I learned to love even when someone does not deserve to be loved. It is when I learned how You love me. While I was learning these things, I remained faithful. I was serving and receiving nothing in return; however, I pressed on. Hearing these words, as I was looking at rainbow clouds, overwhelmed me with emotion. I remember choking on a tear and hearing, *It is over.* The horrible trial I was smack in the middle of was over. I did not know why or have any reason to believe that the trial was over. The only thing I had was the words and a feeling. When I got home that day, I could not shake the feeling. In the afternoon, I stepped on my front porch and I pondered the van ride and my conversation with You, Jesus. I remember looking up and seeing a complete rainbow. It was bright and clear and whole. I stood in awe. I believed You were making me a promise. I knew You were faithful and if You were making me a promise You would keep it.

At that time, I did not know what it meant. I wanted to know for sure. I had to know. I remember running into the house and grabbing my Bible. I was searching and longing for answers. I was hoping. I turned to Zephaniah 3:17. I will never forget the words I read. "The Lord your God is with you, he is mighty to save. He will take great delight in you, he will quiet you with his love, he will rejoice over you with singing." I continued reading:

> The sorrows for the appointed feasts I will remove from you; they are a burden and a reproach to you. At that time, I will deal with all who oppressed you. At that time, I will gather you; at that time, I will bring you home. I will give you honor and praise among all the peoples of the earth when I restore your fortunes before your very eyes, says the Lord.
>
> Zephaniah 3:18–20

I continued into Haggai 1 and 2. Words were jumping off the page. Highlighted. Spoken to me. *For I am with you. Do not fear. I will fill this house with glory. I will grant peace. From this day on I will bless you. I have chosen you.*

The picture of the whole rainbow still sits in my Bible as a reminder of Your promise and Your faithfulness. Zephaniah and Haggai have pencil outlining Your promises to me with a date next to them in my Bible. Tucked away cleverly hidden behind the pages is a small strip of paper recounting Your goodness to me. It was, in fact, over. You delivered me then and You will deliver me now. You kept Your promise to me then and You will keep Your promise to me now. Thank You that You are the same yesterday, today and forever. I can count on You always because You never change. I love You and I will trust You this time too.

"Jesus Christ the same yesterday, and today, and forever" (Heb. 13:8).

I have set my rainbow in the clouds, and it will be the sign of the covenant between me and the earth. Whenever I bring clouds over the earth and the rainbow appears in the clouds, I will remember my covenant between me and you and all living creatures of every kind. Never again will the waters become a flood to destroy all life. Whenever the rainbow appears in the clouds, I will see it and remember the everlasting covenant between God and all living creatures of every kind on the earth.

So, God said to Noah, "This is the sign of the covenant I have established between me and all life on the earth."

Genesis 9:13–17

FOURTEEN

April 17, 2017
Dear Jesus,

It is Easter morning. The sun is shining, birds are chirping, and the grass is green. Oh so green. I love the smells and sounds of spring. My house is a mess as we prepare for church, but I do not care. Memories are being made as my family does life together. I look at their faces. Gratefulness spills over into the day. I whisper quiet thanks for the beautiful lives you have given me. Joy is beginning to prick daily life again, but the pain is still bubbling underneath.

Butterflies are fluttering outside my window and I think I might even have a smile on my face. Brandon asks me to send out an email for work and I grab my phone and begin to search for the needed email in my inbox. The email was gone so I began to type in different combinations of the person's name to compose the email. No luck. I opened my trash folder to find it. Just like that my morning is changed.

It has been seven months and I am still grieving. As the words entered my existence yet again my insides begin to burn. I tried to delete the words without reading anything, but it was too late. My heart felt as if it might burst as I saw words that hurt me to my core. These words play over and over in my mind.

I began to speak life. I began to pray quietly in my van. Please cover my mind, Jesus. Thank You that You love me. Please let any thoughts that are not of You leave. I only want to hear one voice. Amen. Peace entered as I looked to You. As I worshipped in church, I desired to worship You with all my heart and soul. With my eyes shut I envisioned myself standing and singing with my arms reaching the heavens. These words left my mouth:

There in the ground His body lay, light of the world by darkness slain, then bursting forth in glorious day, up from the grave he rose again, and as He stands in victory, sin's curse has lost its grip on me, for I am his and he is mine, bought with the precious blood of Christ, no guilt in life, no fear in death, this is the power of Christ in me, from life's first cry to final breath, Jesus commands my destiny, no power of hell, no scheme of man, can ever pluck me from his hand, till he returns or calls me home, here in the power of Christ I'll stand.

"In Christ Alone"

You stand in victory. I am Yours and You are mine. Jesus, You reached down from on high and took hold of me. As I continue running this race marked out for me it feels more like a marathon. After church, I started feeling better. I was with my family eating Easter dinner. The atmosphere was filled with light conversation and then the topic of birthdays came up. Sweet Ella Rose chimed in and told everyone that her birthday was June 18, 2010. She continued telling everyone that this year was going to be really, special because it was on Father's Day this year. She then pushed back her chair and ran over to Brandon at the end of the table. It was such a sweet sight. Brandon grabbed hold of her, pulled her in and they kissed. I love that Ella has a dad who is so loving and real. I love that I am married to this man, but amid this overwhelming joy, tears began to well in my eyes. I felt the pain of my loss. I have no dad. Pain began to bubble up from deep within. I began to run again.

Jesus, my race continues, and it is hard and painful. I am choosing life. Please help me remember Your truth. I have a Father. A perfect father who loves me. You say, I am beautiful, I am protected, I am chosen, I am family and I am Yours.

When I got home later that afternoon, I came up to my computer to empty my trash folder. The folder contained death. Words that hurt me deeply. Thank You, Jesus, that Your word is flawless. This

Easter I have hope and I will cling to life producing words until You return. You are my ultimate healer. One day I will be healed completely, but until then I will keep my eyes on You and Your word.

"The tongue has the power of life and death, and those who love it will eat its fruit" (Prov. 18:21).

"The thief comes only to steal and kill and destroy; I have come that they may have life and have it to the full" (John 10:10).

"He reached down from on high and took hold of me; he drew me out of deep waters" (Ps. 18:6).

"As for God, his way is perfect: The LORD's word is flawless; he shields all who take refuge in him" (Ps. 18:30).

"Let the king be enthralled by your beauty; honor him, for he is your lord" (Ps. 45:11).

"He will not let your foot slip—he who watches over you will not slumber" (Ps. 121:3).

"You did not choose me, but I chose you and appointed you so that you might go and bear fruit, fruit that will last—and so that whatever you ask in my name the Father will give you" (John 15:16).

"Consequently, you are no longer foreigners and strangers, but fellow citizens with God's people and also members of his household" (Eph. 2:19).

"But now, this is what the LORD says—he who created you, Jacob, he who formed you, Israel: 'Do not fear, for I have redeemed you; I have summoned you by name; you are mine'" (Isa. 43:1).

"But he was pierced for our transgressions, he was crushed for our iniquities; the punishment that brought us peace was on him, and by his wounds we are healed" (Isa. 53:5).

"Yet for us there is but one God, the Father, from whom all things came and for whom we live; and there is but one Lord, Jesus Christ, through whom all things came and through whom we live" (1 Cor. 8:6).

> Therefore, since we are surrounded by such a great cloud of witnesses, let us throw off everything that hinders and the sin that so easily entangles. And let us run with perseverance the race marked out for us.
>
> Hebrews 12:1

FIFTEEN

June 11, 2017
Dear Jesus,

Something has been on my heart. Why do I do the things I do? Is it a checklist? Is it to make You happy? Do I do it because I feel as if I need to? Jesus, I want my heart to be soft, pliable. I want what matters to You to matter to me. I want You to mold me and shape me to be like You. I want to hunger and thirst for Your righteousness. I want to see sin how You see sin. Not for me, but to glorify the Father. I know what matters to You is my heart. You want me to be in a right relationship with You and then go out and love others. As I read Your word, I realize You are everywhere. You are near and want to be active in my daily life. Over and over as I write one theme persists: You are faithful, You are near, and You hear me.

Recently something happened that made my heart ache. Two lost sheep returned home. They settled back into the familiar wood pew. I watched them worship. It was beautiful. She had a smile on her face, and she stood close by her husband's side as the piano played in the background. He stood tall with his hands raised to the one and only You. Joy poked my heart for a moment. It was quickly replaced by something raw and dark. A bold statement was broadcast before we broke bread and the church ran those lost sheep out the door. Who knows our hearts but You, Lord? I am so confused. Aren't we all unworthy to come to the table? I continue to wrestle with this. The language used was biblically referenced. To me, it felt like unloving, unforgiving judgment so I am asking You what is next. What do You want me to do?

I am going to follow You, Jesus. I am not going to follow You with a checklist, but with my heart and Your word. It is my heart movement. I pray, read Your word, and I see You move. You led me to Luke 15:4–7:

> Suppose one of you has a hundred sheep and loses one of them. Doesn't he leave the ninety-nine in the open country and go after the lost sheep until he finds it? And when he finds it, he joyfully puts it on his shoulders and goes home. Then he calls his friends and neighbors together and says, 'Rejoice with me; I have found my lost sheep.' I tell you that in the same way there will be more rejoicing in heaven over one sinner who repents than over the ninety-nine righteous persons who do not need to repent.

I continue my walk with You. I know I do not have all the answers, I am just a sheep; however, I hope that when people see me, they will see You and love will be the loudest sound they hear.

Sunday my car pulled into the parking lot lined with many cars. Brandon backed into a space so we could easily escape the traffic after church. My family entered the sanctuary lined with chairs and I see the stage up ahead. We took our seats. Am I doing the right thing? I do not know, but my heart moves, I pray, I read Your word and I see You move. One of the first songs we sang is, "King of My Heart" which You know I have been singing repeatedly. I worshipped wholeheartedly. Then the pastor prayed these words: "He has shown you, O mortal, what is good. And what does the Lord require of you? To act justly and to love mercy and to walk humbly with your God" (Micah 6:8). You know I have been clinging to this verse for the last nine months. Knowing how to navigate this trial is so hard. These words guide me and teach me Your ways, Lord. Peace came as the sermon continued in Isaiah and then the pastor asked a question about manipulation and how it makes us feel. I thought to myself, *is this really happening?* The pastor continued to talk about manipulation, and I thought, *this is my life.* How can he know? I know he does not, but Spirit does. I know that You are speaking to me. I know I am in the right place at the right time and then the pastor gave another example. A puzzle. A literal puzzle. My favorite show was the puzzle. An unlikely puzzle. An unexpected puzzle. Jesus, You know me. You are near and love me intimately. Every detail of me.

All people are sinners unworthy to come to the table. All people are dirty. You are the one who makes us clean. You know my heart. I do not want to follow a religion. I want to follow You Jesus. I know You care about my heart. Thank You for being faithful, near, and hearing me when I call out to You. I love being with You, listening to You and following You. I know I cannot see You, but I know You exist. I am in awe of You, creator of all things. I am giving up religion and sitting with You, the one who loves and will teach me to love.

"He said to them, "You are the ones who justify yourselves in the eyes of others, but God knows your hearts. What people value highly is detestable in God's sight" (Luke 16:15).

"And he who searches our hearts knows the mind of the Spirit, because the Spirit intercedes for God's people in accordance with the will of God" (Rom. 8:27).

"'The multitude of your sacrifices—what are they to me?' says the LORD" (Isa. 1:11).

"Jesus replied: 'Love the Lord your God with all your heart and with all your soul and with all your mind'" (Matt. 22:37).

"When they saw the courage of Peter and John and realized that they were unschooled, ordinary men, they were astonished, and they took note that these men had been with Jesus" (Acts 4:13).

"Call to me and I will answer you and tell you great and unsearchable things you do not know" (Jer. 33:3).

"HOPE"

Heavy dark clouds rolling in
sneaking in like a lion
looking for someone to devour
knocked down
fallen in a pit
emotions well inside
sadness
anger
anguish
darkness overwhelms
buried alive
clawing
scratching
pleading
hand raised
reaching out
hoping
in the stillness
a speck of light
meeting me there
right where I was
coming in like a flood
He reached down from on high and took hold of me
and drew me out
memories fill my mind
a rush of love
sweet morning sister chats
rainbow cloud through glasses
a steeple in the distance
nineties music

Fifteen

Swedish Fish
hip-hop
pretty packaging in the mail
tutus and nail polish
cartwheels
diving board flips
wheelies
line throwing
yellow belly
water rushing
balloon tossing
laughing
wet grass in your toes
toad goodbyes
hand holding
ice cream stop
tooth pulling
drink offering
truth sharing
bear hug, sobbing
new life
seed planting
a perfect word
the perfect time
rough hands on my neck
confirmation
blonde raccoon
wild daisies
black berries
cool breeze
coffee making
worshipping chain

mating pairs of orange and black
engine revving
brisk morning
fawns in the valley
doe on the hill
mercies are new every morning (Lam. 3:22)
the Light shine in the darkness
the darkness has not overcome it (John 1:5)

"BREATHE"

I breathe you in
I breathe you out

JESUS

Hold me
Hide me

I breathe you in
I breathe you out

JESUS

Infuse me with joy
Instill me with peace

I breathe you in
I breathe you out

JESUS

Build me roots
Bear my pain

I breathe you in
I breathe you out

JESUS

Show me Your glory
Still my soul

I breathe you in
I breathe you out

JESUS

Fill me with hope
Fan my flame

I breathe you in
I breathe you out

JESUS

Quench my thirst
Quiet my mind

I breathe you in
I breathe you out

JESUS

Satisfy my longing
Saturate my life

I breathe you in
I breathe you out

JESUS

SIXTEEN

July 27, 2017
Dear Jesus,

I am in a valley. I feel tormented. I am struggling and feeling hopeless. The struggle is real. Have my eyes slipped, Jesus? When my eyes are on You, I am victorious. When I take my eyes off You, I sink. When I am looking at my circumstances, I forget Your truth. You have already won my battle. Every battle You have won. You lived a sinless, perfect life and died on the cross for me. I should not be weary or hopeless or defeated. You have won my battle. Your battle. I believe in You, have faith in You and am seated with You in the heavenly realm. Thank You for never leaving me alone. Thank You for the Holy Spirit and guiding me in the way I should go.

This valley is deep and long. My faith is growing, and I am learning more about You. This chipping and shaping my character to mirror You is painful, but knowing You is a true treasure. No matter how gruesome this trial gets, I am seeing there are always hidden jewels. Your jewels are precious. Some of the precious jewels I have collected this past year are: a humble heart, a deeper relationship with Brandon, restoration of my brokenness from my childhood, an intimate relationship with You, an earnest prayer life, deep, narrow-road friendships and the life lesson on how to put my armor on. I know the battle is not mine. This trial I am in is not the problem. The person who hurt me is not my enemy. I have learned that my struggle is not against flesh and blood, but against the rulers, against the authorities, against the powers of this dark world and against the spiritual forces of evil in the heavenly realms.

My valley keeps going deeper and deeper. I continue to think I cannot go any further, but I trudge on. This trial is hurting not only me, but my family. When the pain reaches my children, I think no, *not my children.* Why them? God, grow me, but not at the expense of my kids. I know it is not my place to judge. I know my thoughts are not Your thoughts and Your ways are so much higher than mine. Help me trust You this time too. I know You are good, strong and there is no one like You. I know this because Your word says so and Your word is truth. As I walk in this unknown place, I will trust You, Jesus. I trust Your plan is good and for me. I will trust You to work out everything for my good. I trust You will unite everything in heaven and earth to Yourself.

Last week an event happened that shook me to the core. It created such fear and anxiety right in the center of my heart. My heart raced. Nausea filled my mouth. Lies filled my mind and my eyes fell to my circumstances and once again I began to sink. In my own strength, my mind planned. What can I do? Do this. Do that. Make this happen. Make that happen. I took matters into my own hands. My own way. The thoughts ran rampant in my mind. But You. I breathed You in and I breathed You out. I looked up. You reminded me the battle is not mine, but Yours. You are taking care of me. You gave me weapons that work, Your word, and the power of prayer. Once again, I began my love walk with You, my Savior. I spoke truth. I trust You. My confidence is in You alone. You are holy. You are worthy. Thank You for Your plan and drawing me close.

Last night I laid in bed reading the Psalms. The words washed over me and flooded me with peace that surpassed all understanding. My chest pain began to diminish as I laid with You. I then read Ephesians 6 and read about my struggle and how to put my armor on, again and again. I prayed that You would reveal the ultimate truth. I prayed You would enlighten my eyes so I could see the hope to which You have called me. I prayed while I slept. In the night I saw rainbows, hearts and victory written in the sky. I am holding on to these promises, love, and hope.

Sixteen

As my eyes slowly opened this morning, I smelled fresh brewed coffee. A love offering from Brandon, but there was more. You heard me. You revealed truth this morning. A painful, beautiful jewel wrapped in victory.

He said: Listen, King Jehoshaphat and all who live in Judah and Jerusalem! This is what the LORD says to you: Do not be afraid or discouraged because of this vast army. For the battle is not yours, but God's.

2 Chronicles 20:15

Finally, be strong in the Lord and in his mighty power. Put on the full armor of God, so that you can take your stand against the devil's schemes. For our struggle is not against flesh and blood, but against the rulers, against the authorities, against the powers of this dark world and against the spiritual forces of evil in the heavenly realms. Therefore, put on the full armor of God, so that when the day of evil comes, you may be able to stand your ground, and after you have done everything, to stand. Stand firm then, with the belt of truth buckled around your waist, with the breastplate of righteousness in place, and with your feet fitted with the readiness that comes from the gospel of peace. In addition to all this, take up the shield of faith, with which you can extinguish all the flaming arrows of the evil one. Take the helmet of salvation and the sword of the Spirit, which is the word of God.

Ephesians 6:10–17

For my thoughts are not your thoughts, neither are your ways my ways, declares the LORD. As the heavens are higher than the earth, so are my ways higher than your ways and my thoughts than your thoughts.

Isaiah 55:8–9

"The weapons we fight with are not the weapons of the world. On the contrary, they have divine power to demolish strongholds" (2 Cor. 10:4).

"For the word of God is alive and active. Sharper than any double-edged sword..." (Heb. 4:12).

SEVENTEEN

July 29, 2017
Dear Jesus,

I keep hearing the same words. *Patient endurance is where you need to be. You need to patiently endure. I am training you in patient endurance.* These words continue to poke me. Everywhere I turn I hear them. See them. It started last Saturday, then in Sunday's sermon, and finally, today in my daily devotional. I have been here before, in the waiting stage. This is the part where I want to give up, quit, curl up, and hide; however, when I sit still, I can hear Your voice encouraging me to march on. I do not want to move forward in a forlorn way but help me move triumphantly, Jesus. I know You will deliver me from this place because You are the deliverer. I know You will restore me because You are the Father of restoration. You take broken things and make them beautiful. You take bad things and turn them to good. I will praise You because You are God.

I am hurting. I am being stretched, pulled, and prodded. I am suffering. I then began to think of You, Jesus, and how You suffered for my sake. You did not deserve any of it, but You willingly took the punishment for me. You were forsaken so that I would never have to be. Help me learn obedience through my suffering as You did. Help me remember this beautiful truth, that because You died for me, I will never be in this suffering alone. Thank You for using this suffering and hardship for my good. I know You are making a beautiful masterpiece of my life for Your glory. Thank You for taking all the good, all the bad, all the pretty and all the ugly and making something more beautiful than I could ever hope for or imagine.

I have been in the waiting stage before. I remember listening to all the voices surrounding me, all the noise in my head, all the directions and instructions of what I should or should not do. I remember listening to all the doubts, discouragement, and disappointment in my personal choices. I listened to all the lies, but during that time of suffering is where I learned to trust, tune it out, sing in the storm, walk by faith and not by sight. I learned how to follow You, Jesus. I did not have to listen to the news, what people thought or Christian leaders. I could follow You and Your word. I trusted You during every step of my suffering and deliverance. You became so real to me at that time in my life. You were involved in every choice and every detail and brought us to a place of abundantly more. Help me believe and trust You this time too.

I am choosing You. I am choosing life. I am choosing to trust and run this race marked out for me. I am choosing to see past the struggle keeping my eyes on You, my prize. I am choosing You over every lemon, puddle, dark and yucky spot. In the suffering is the most beautiful spot. It is the space where hope lives. It is where Your words come to life and where I believe You will do immeasurably more than I will ask or imagine. I am resting in this space. This beautiful spacious place. In the stillness with my beautiful Savior waiting to see Your marvelous masterpiece revealed.

"And the God of all grace, who called you to his eternal glory in Christ, after you have suffered a little while, will himself restore you and make you strong, firm, and steadfast" (1 Pet. 5:8).

"Son though he was, he learned obedience from what he suffered" (Heb. 5:8).

"Blessed is she who has believed that the Lord would fulfill his promises to her" (Luke 1:45).

"For we live by faith, not by sight" (2 Cor. 5:7).

SEVENTEEN

Therefore, since we are surrounded by such a great cloud of witnesses, let us throw off everything that hinders and the sin that so easily entangles. And let us run with perseverance the race marked out for us.

Hebrews 12:1

"After Job had prayed for his friends, the LORD restored his fortunes and gave him twice as much as he had before" (Job 42:10).

"Now to him who is able to do immeasurably more than all we ask or imagine, according to his power that is at work within us" (Eph. 3:20).

EIGHTEEN

September 11, 2017
Dear Jesus,

I am running and racing. I am running from one thing to the next. I am praying, praying, praying, urgently. Is there any rest for the weary? I am so weary. Is it possible to trust You, Jesus, and then start run, run, running and race, race, racing again in my prayer life? How many times have I heard the verse, "Come to me, all you who are weary and burdened, and I will give you rest" (Matt. 11:28)? How many times have I tried to apply it to my life? I think I am beginning to get it. A small nugget of how Your word is intended. You are showing me something new. You are revealing to me the place where You want me to be. Held in Your arms.

I struggle with this balance. It is a fine balance. This Christian walk. This Jesus following. I know it is good to pray and to pray continually, but I know You want to walk through each day with me. Lately, I have been caught up in praying a certain way. I find myself in this place where I want my family to go deep with You and I think I need to pray all the right prayers so that Brandon has an intimate relationship with You. I pray frantically for my children, so they have an intimate relationship with You. Today. Not tomorrow. Today. If things start going the wrong way or I am not liking what I am seeing in Brandon or the kids, I think I did not cover them in prayer enough. I did not pray the right words, the right verses, the right way. Can it be, Jesus? Am I trying to control people, my circumstances and even my relationship with You? As the questions roll around in my brain, I hear You whisper, "I am doing something new. Trust me."

Can I even make an idol out of prayer? This makes me so sad.

Our world is so broken and twisted. Am I thinking too deep? Am I thinking too much? I am curious so I looked up the definition of the word "idol." The definition of an idol is:

1. A representation or symbol of an object of worship; a false god or
2. An object of extreme devotion.

When I think of an idol, I think of anything that is put before You. Things like material objects, sports, hobbies, work, exercise, and food. Have I become so confused that I even distort the most beautiful thing, my prayer life with You? As I read the definitions and prayed with You it begins to become clearer to me. It is not so much an idol as it is control. In this fallen world sin so easily entangles me. Even in the things I believe I am doing for You and for Your good.

I am lying in bed with my prayer binder last night. I am covering Brandon, my kids, my trials, my family, my friends, my longings, and desires with prayers using Your word. I am running, running, running. I am racing, racing, racing. I am praying, praying, praying. And then the tears fell. I cannot do this. This life is hard. I am in a lot of pain and this trial is so exhausting. I have so much fear of the unknown and so much sadness. There is so much resting on the outcome of the trial, Your truth. Forgive me for twisting my prayers into something You do not desire of me. I know I should put my armor on and walk through this day with You. I know I should put You first, but I need to release my burdens to Your hands. They are not mine to carry. You know my heart. Thank You for teaching me I do not have to pray a certain way and thank You for completely covering me by Your blood. I am safe and secure. I give up control. I am choosing to rest in You. I want to run with perseverance the race marked out for me keeping my eyes fixed on You, knowing that You are doing the work. I know I can trust You because You are before all things, and in You all things hold together.

I was working out at the gym this morning and I had the most beautiful vision. The moon was hanging in the middle of the vast sky.

Beautiful. Brilliant. Round. Nothing anywhere near it. Just there. And then I heard You, "I am holding the moon. I am holding you. You do not have to work, Kari. Rest my sweet daughter." I know I am suspended by Your mighty hand.

"In his hand are the depths of the earth, and the mountain peaks belong to him" (Ps. 95:4).

"Pray continually" (1 Thess. 5:17).

> Therefore, since we are surrounded by such a great cloud of witnesses, let us throw off everything that hinders and the sin that so easily entangles. And let us run with perseverance the race marked out for us.
>
> Hebrews 12:1

"He is before all things, and in him all things hold together" (Col. 1:17).

"See, I am doing a new thing! Now it springs up; do you not perceive it? I am making a way in the wilderness and streams in the wasteland" (Isa. 43:19).

NINETEEN

September 12, 2017
Dear Jesus,

I had a dream and I was on a long, narrow hiking trail. It was slightly dark, and the view was short. I could not see what was around the corner. I saw light piercing through the canopy of trees overhead. The trail was sprinkled with colored leaves and acorns that crunched when I stepped. I heard the rustling of the leaves as squirrels moved from branch to branch. I did not feel scared because I knew the path was planned out for me. I was at perfect peace because the trail had a destination.

Thank You that my life has a destination. Thank You for Your perfect plan for my life. Thank You for creating me for purpose and giving me a hope and a future. When I walk with You, Jesus, there is no fear. With You there is only perfect peace because You orchestrate my steps by divine appointment. In my dream, I knew where I was going because the hiking trail had been mapped out for me. An engineer designed where it would go and where it would end. You, Jesus, mapped out my life. You are the creator and the engineer of my life. I am so glad You know where I am going. Thank You for each step and each stage of my life. Help me trust You as I rely on You.

Lord, many times I wonder if I am going the right way. How do I know if I am on the right path? How do I know if I hit a detour? What if I get lost? Then I hear Your voice, "My word is a lamp to guide your feet and a light for your path" (Ps. 119:105). Your word is a map for my life. When I read Your word, I am illuminating the path before me. I know I am at perfect peace because I am on Your narrow road.

Every day I have choices to make. I do not want to go to the right or the left. I do not want to go my way. I want to follow You, Jesus. I will get out my map. I am jumping all in. I am trusting You to do the work. Thank You for equipping me to be everything You created me to be. Thank You that when I mess up, You are right here waiting to help and guide me. I cannot see where I am going, but I do see Your light piercing through the darkness. Thank You that as I read Your word, pray, and rest in You, You are faithful to show the way. I will live by faith and not by sight as You work out everything for my good.

"Now faith is confidence in what we hope for and assurance about what we do not see" (Heb. 11:1).

"For I know the plans I have for you," declares the LORD, "plans to prosper you and not to harm you, plans to give you hope and a future" (Jer. 29:11).

"But small is the gate and narrow the road that leads to life, and only a few find it" (Matt. 7:14).

"For we live by faith, not by sight" (2 Cor. 5:7).

"Do not turn to the right or the left; keep your foot from evil" (Prov. 4:27).

TWENTY

October 3, 2017
Dear Jesus,

It finally happened. I finally ended up not just broken, but completely broken. Humble. Palms open with nothing to offer. My life has been shattered in a million pieces. The only desire that was left behind was a mission for truth. I know that the only thing in this life that truly matters is a life full of love, joy, peace, forbearance, kindness, goodness, faithfulness, gentleness, and self-control. My broken life has collided with Your redemptive plan.

I know that You love the humble and the weak. You love the broken and the bruised. You love sinners and You sent Your one and only son to die for them. You are close to the brokenhearted and save those who are crushed in spirit. Broken people are ripe for kingdom service because they know their need for a Savior, and they realize they can do nothing in their own strength. They long for a life only You can provide, and they desire what You desire, truth and grace. Broken people long to tell a hurting world the good news, that there is hope. You offer a life of abundance and freedom. We have a glorious inheritance waiting for us in a place that will never die. We have a Father who tells us we are blessed, chosen, loved, wanted, forgiven, saved, sealed, free, created for a purpose and Yours.

Words I have carried around my neck for years such as rebellious, defiant, secretive, quitter, and selfish have been finally taken off permanently. I have replaced it with one word, forgiven. At one time these words may have defined me, but not any longer. I know I was other things as well. Some great things even; however, these words carried the greatest burden. Somehow, someway You chose

81

me despite these flaws. I love how You see me and how You can use broken people like me. I love how I can look back over my life now and see so many mistakes I made, so many hidden secrets, and so much sin, and yet see You use all of it for my good even years later. It is astounding how much You love Your children. All my wrong turns, right turns, the bumps in the road, and You used all of it. It is all interwoven, messy, and beautiful.

As my will merged into Your will, You began to pick up the pieces of my broken life. You knew exactly how the pieces fit back together. I did not even know where I left them, or which ones were missing. I surely did not know which pieces were broken or how to fix them. I am thankful You know me from beginning to end. My life I imagine looks like a mirage of colorful, fragmented pieces fitting together seamlessly into the frame of a beautiful kaleidoscope. It does not look or feel the same as it did before because You are the God of immeasurably more. You added all the ingredients necessary for a full life and breathed on every fragmented piece love and truth.

> Brothers and sisters think of what you were when you were called. Not many of you were wise by human standards; not many were influential; not many were of noble birth. But God chose the foolish things of the world to shame the wise; God chose the weak things of the world to shame the strong. God chose the lowly things of this world and the despised things—and the things that are not—to nullify the things that are, so that no one may boast before him. It is because of him that you are in Christ Jesus, who has become for us wisdom from God—that is, our righteousness, holiness, and redemption. Therefore, as it is written: "Let the one who boasts boast in the Lord."
> 1 Corinthians 1:26–31

"But many who are first will be last, and the last first" (Mark 10:31).

"God opposes the proud but shows favor to the humble" (James 4:6).

"For the LORD takes delight in his people; he crowns the humble with victory" (Ps. 149:4).

> But he said to me, "My grace is sufficient for you, for my power is made perfect in weakness." Therefore, I will boast all the more gladly about my weaknesses, so that Christ's power may rest on me. That is why, for Christ's sake, I delight in weaknesses, in insults, in hardships, in persecutions, in difficulties. For when I am weak, then I am strong.
>
> 2 Corinthians 12:9–10

"But the fruit of the Spirit is love, joy, peace, forbearance, kindness, goodness, faithfulness, gentleness, and self-control" (Gal. 5:22–23).

"A bruised reed he will not break, and a smoldering wick he will not snuff out, till he has brought justice through to victory" (Matt. 12:20).

"The LORD is close to the brokenhearted and saves those who are crushed in spirit" (Ps. 34:18).

"For all have sinned and fall short of the glory of God" (Rom. 3:23).

"But God demonstrates his own love for us in this: While we were still sinners, Christ died for us" (Rom. 5:8).

"And we know that in all things God works for the good of those who love him, who have been called according to his purpose" (Rom. 8:28).

TWENTY-ONE

October 4, 2017
Dear Jesus,

I have been hearing You for the last few days. You are whispering the same thing. I know I have been ignoring You. I do not know why, but I am filled with trepidation. I do not know what You are going to say to me. I do not know what You are going to ask of me. I feel like I have nothing left to give. I do not want to go deeper, but Your whispers keep coming. Come. Come to the carpet. Palms up. Sit. It is not hard for me to find other things to do. I have mountains of laundry, dishes, piles everywhere, bills, work, investing, cooking, exercising, phone calls, and writing. The list could go on for days. I have been canceling the to-do-list this week and I have been spending more time at home. I can hear You telling me to rest. I can hear You telling me to trust. I do not know why, but the urge to do more is ever present. I think I should be doing more, but as I begin to trudge up the mountain of other things to do, I hear You louder and louder. Rest. Come. Come to the carpet. Palms up. Sit.

Okay, soon, I think. Then I notice hair balls flying under the bench when I walk by, smeared handprints on my window, the phone ringing in the background and I think, *maybe later*. You know I am still praying and reading Your word. I am still walking through this day with You, why do I have to go to the carpet? Something big is stirring in my heart, but I do not know what it is. I am feeling heartbroken over our fallen world. The Las Vegas shooting happened a few days ago and every time I see footage or pray for Your people tears fall. I see the wreckage of all the hurricanes and earthquakes and I turn my head away not being able to bear the scene. I hear harsh

85

words spoken by my children, Brandon, and me and I think, sin. Come, Lord. Come, Lord Jesus. I fall asleep thinking about sin and brokenness and yet I am feeling inspired. But, what?

As my eyes open, I hear You say, "Come. Come to the carpet. Palms up. Sit." I decide in the shower today is the day I will come to the carpet. I will come right after I take the kids to school. Yet I come home to the dust bunnies, dishes, and piles and I think I have to come to the carpet with my full attention so I take care of these things so I can concentrate on You, Lord, with no distractions. I am doing my chores, making dinner, talking on the phone and I feel nervous. The time is near. I am going to the carpet.

I grab a piece of paper and a pen and sit crisscross on the carpet. I shut my eyes and lay my palms facing up on my legs. My mind is busy. There is so much clutter up there. Why can't I shut out the noise for one minute so I can hear what You must tell me already? This is so hard. I cannot shut up. Prayers are swirling around up there, noise, so much noise, verses, to-do-lists, and garbage are up there. I breathe in. I am going to tell You about this experience. My palms are up, and random thoughts are coming in like a flood. Lord, please quiet my mind. And then there was pure silence. I heard the wind in the trees outside my window. It was calm. I sat still longer and still nothing happened. Wind. Trees. I heard the birds singing. I felt peace. I asked You to shine Your light into me and cleanse me. I felt light, warm, and like a burden was lifted. And then here it came. You displayed my idols. You pegged them one at a time. You illuminated all of them. I began to pray for healing physically, emotionally, and spiritually. I then sat in silence. The only noise I could hear was the trees blowing in the wind. I asked You, "Lord, what do You want from me?" Instead of hearing You, I heard what I wanted. I want restoration and blessing. My tears spilled out, ugly with my arms raised. I sat and quietly cried. After I finished crying You showed me three beautiful people who are on my heart. This was so plain, true, and pure. I lifted them all up to You, Lord. My heart continued to stir. I wondered if I could ask You what I wanted to ask You. I did. I laid my heart's desire bare before You, Lord. I heard nothing but pure silence. There were no words, just the sound of the trees rustling in the wind. *Is that all?* I wondered. I stood up and walked off the carpet. I did not hear clear direction from You one way or another. You did not reveal to me some master plan You want me to take part in; however, You did show me plainly what is on my heart. I know I do not have to pray a certain way. You exposed my heart in Your presence. I know now healing comes from being still in the presence of You, Lord. Next time I hear, "Come. Come to the carpet. Palms up. Sit," I will eagerly go back to another carpet ride with You.

"Come to me, all you who are weary and burdened, and I will give you rest" (Matt. 11:28).

"And he who searches our hearts knows the mind of the Spirit, because the Spirit intercedes for God's people in accordance with the will of God" (Rom. 8:27).

TWENTY-TWO

October 9, 2017
Dear Jesus,

I was thinking about words I penned on a picture frame fifteen years ago.

"You are the wind beneath my wings." Love, Kari

At the time I had them engraved, I believed them. Last year when my world was uprooted, I realized these words were not true. One tragic event left me deflated like a balloon. In one moment, all the wind beneath my wings was gone. I was plummeting to the earth below until You steadied my fall. I know now that people are not the wind beneath my wings. No matter how hard people try, they will always let me down. The truth is You are the only person that will never let me down.

Jesus, I am tired. Many days I am weary, and I cry out to You, "How long, Lord?" Every day I pick myself up and move forward because You are renewing my strength. You are not just the wind beneath my wings, but You are the one who is carrying me. I know with You I can soar on wings like eagles. I know that I can run and not grow weary and I can walk and not faint. When I try to move forward in my own strength I fail every time. I become tired and weary easily. When I spend time with You, I am renewed. I have found healing, strength, and restoration come from sitting with You, not serving more, reading my Bible more, or doing more work. When I sit with You, Your light permeates the deepest parts of my body leaving me whole. I know that serving more is great and I want to do this. I know that reading Your word is great and I want to do this too. I know that working hard is great and I want to do this as well; however, if I am not spending time with You, I will fail at all these great things.

Why is it so hard to sit in the quiet with You? I can sit with a book, the computer, my phone, a drink, a snack, and a movie in the quiet. Thank You for teaching me how to rest in You. I love Your stillness, peace, strength, and power. I know I am still learning how to do this well. It is extremely uncomfortable, but it is becoming more comfortable each day I choose to sit, listen, and follow. I do not want to be the kind of Christian who has my salvation but misses out on a little piece of heaven here on earth. You are here today. You are with me and alive today. Somedays You are the only beauty I see. My days are filled with endless to-do-lists, drama in the neighborhood, fighting in the van, unsatisfied customers, and broken relationships. When I sit with You, I experience healing, strength, and restoration. I see hope for tomorrow.

The memory of the words I penned still hurt. They bring up many painful thoughts and memories; however, I do not like to push my feelings down. I want to expose them as painful as they may be. When I share my pain with You, I allow You to heal me and fill in the broken places with Your love. I share Your goodness because it brings You glory and what Satan meant for harm You use for my good to restore me from the inside out. You are the wind beneath my wings.

"And we know that in all things God works for the good of those who love him, who have been called according to his purpose" (Rom. 8:28).

> Even youths grow tired and weary, and young men stumble and fall; but those who hope in the LORD will renew their strength. They will soar on wings like eagles; they will run and not grow weary. They will walk and not be faint.
>
> Isaiah 40:30–31

TWENTY-THREE

October 11, 2017
Dear Jesus,

If You asked my family what my favorite drink is, they would answer unanimously. Diet Coke. Just typing the words make me smile. I love it! Every drop of it. The fizz. The taste. Everything. You know how many times I have tried to drop this habit. Sometimes I have made it a long time, but I always fall back and start sipping this delicious piece of heaven. Does everyone fall back to what is comfortable and what the flesh likes?

I have a confession to make. Diet Coke is not the only thing I am struggling with. I have been binging on food and drink. Diet Coke is my drink of preference, but I love drinking. I love having something in my hand that tastes so good going down. It satisfies me for a few minutes, but soon after I am looking for my next fix. If it is not a drink, it is food. I love food that is crunchy, salty, and sweet and even better yet, a little bit of both. Crunching and sipping is my kind of life; however, it has been on my heart lately that I am trying to fill something deep inside me that cannot be filled with bread alone. These things always satisfy me for a little while, but shortly after the feeling fades and I am looking for my next fix with new guilt intact.

Binging. I am a binger. If it is not drink and food, exercise would be next for me. I always go a little too far with everything, taking it to the extreme, and never being satisfied with the outcome. If I am spending time on these things, I do not have time to focus on what is important: You and these empty holes inside of me. I know that drink, food, and exercise are not bad. I know that these things can be enjoyable, rewarding, and healthy even. Many times, when I am running or on an

91

elliptical machine, I spend time with You in prayer and worship which is so good and healthy. What You are showing me is much bigger than this. It is my focus. My lens is out of whack. I have been looking for healing, restoration, and satisfaction from things other than You.

Lately, the binging has become worse because I am still suffering. I think I am trying to satisfy my hurting heart, trying to feel better and looking for joy and peace. I know this and have written about it. I know that You are the one who satisfies, heals, and restores. Slowly, slowly my soul is getting it. I need to sit with You. I need to rest with You. I need to bring my trials into Your light with my palms up. I need to tell You about how I am struggling and hurting and let Your light fill my holes with brilliance only You can provide. My soul craves You. My soul thirsts for You in a dry and weary land where there is no water. Your word is the nutrition my soul needs. I will live on every word that comes from Your mouth. Next time I feel the need to fill my mouth with drink or food, I will think before I fill. Next time I run to the gym, I will think before I run. What am I hungering for? What is it I am craving? I have a feeling I am craving something more than bread. I will feast on nuggets of truth and then sit with You, the only one who can satisfy my binging soul.

"You, God, are my God, earnestly I seek you; I thirst for you, my whole being longs for you, in a dry and parched land where there is no water" (Ps. 63:1).

"It is written: 'Man shall not live on bread alone, but on every word that comes from the mouth of God'" (Matt. 4:4).

"Everyone's toil is for their mouth, yet their appetite is never satisfied" (Eccl. 6:7).

"After he has suffered, he will see the light of life and be satisfied; by his knowledge, my righteous servant will justify many, and he will bear their iniquities" (Isa. 53:11).

TWENTY-FOUR

October 18, 2017
Dear Jesus,

Two times in the last week I have had a picture in my mind. I am nearing the top of the mountain. I am three quarters of the way there. *Could it be?* In the beginning of this trial, sadness plagued me. My boundary was set in place and darkness followed. I was not prepared for the darkness, long days, quietness, and sadness. Will I ever get off my couch? Will I ever stop crying? When will my energy come back? Will it ever? The life has been sucked out of me.

You have asked me to do hard, unthinkable things. I have never been fond of boundaries. I like to dangle in them always crossing over to the other side. I have always liked to push the limit, but You know that about me. There are some people who see everything in black and white, but not me. I love the gray area. As I have matured, I have learned that boundaries are put in place to keep me safe. This is what Your word has taught me and what I teach my children. I know that You do not set boundaries to hurt us, but the very opposite, to protect us and give us freedom. I still love to linger in gray areas with surface things, but I have learned to create boundaries for every important life sustaining conviction. I will still wear my "holy" jeans to church (gray area); however, when someone intends to lie, manipulate, or harm me, I will mosey on back behind the fence. The difference between the two is one hurts me, and the other does not. Boundaries are critical for my spiritual well-being, as well as physical, emotional, and mental health. I will always choose to stand with You, Jesus, and the truth even if I am the only one left standing. I will not cave with the lies just because it is easier. Sometimes I wish I could brush it under the rug, but when I chose You, I chose to stand for what You stand for, truth. All the boundaries You have helped me secure are created for my protection for my life as Your follower. My boundaries have never been about hurting people, but about protecting me, my family and my love for You and Your word.

As I trudge up the mountain, healing begins one grief emotion after another. Sadness has turned to fear, and the fear has overcome me, yet I am choosing to trust You anyway. I choose to give up personal relationships to stand with You. Fear has been with me at every turn. I have become a prisoner to my own fear, enslaved by the what ifs. For months, fear has been with me, but I know You have been with me too. Your light shines in the darkness and the darkness has not overcome it. Day after day I call to You for protection, healing, and peace. As I walk with You, You strengthen my heart muscle. I am continuing to empty the hurts inside of me to You because You see me and know me. I know that You keep me safe from harm and accusing tongues. You are my shield and refuge. As I continue to pray for healing, You have not only protected me, but You are restoring me from the inside out. As I bring my hurts into Your light You restore them while simultaneously shielding me from the darts of hatred. I continue to grow and am beginning to forgive just as You have forgiven me. Forgiveness has been hard, but day in and day out, I forgive, trusting You as my defender and vindicator. I know that my heart muscle has grown, and I am becoming stronger as each day passes. I am choosing to let go and let You do Your best work.

As minutes turn to hours, hours turn to days and days turn to months something new is beginning to emerge. Peace. It snuck up on me and washed over me. When did it exactly happen? I do not really know, but somewhere along the mountain side. As I walk with You and bare my soul, You do what You do best: restore broken things. Healing and peace must go hand in hand and when You add a little trust and patience things begin to change. I am beginning to soar up the mountainside. I think I can almost see the top. As I begin to trust You more, rest more and sit with You more, the fear begins to subside and transforms into a miraculous peace.

Many emotions have come and gone. Sadness, fear, and peace are at the top of my list. Along with these emotions have been boundaries, forgiveness, and healing. Two things have been critical in my journey of restoration, trust, and patience. Trust and patience have allowed me to go through the days of sadness and fear. Thank You for not leaving me alone in this journey. You are my ultimate healer. Without You I would still be immobile on my couch. I would still be locked in my house paralyzed in fear, but because of You, I am healing and feeling peace which surpasses all understanding. Boundaries, forgiveness, and healing are so closely intertwined. Boundaries have given me the protection I need to forgive and without forgiveness, I would not be healing.

I know this journey is not over by a long shot, but more days than not I am feeling stronger with peace and joy brewing from my insides. I am still having days when things happen that take me back to the hurt and sadness and even the fear, but my heart has been strengthened and I am able to press into You and move forward. Thank You for not leaving me in the valley forever. Thank You for Your mercies which are new every morning. This mountain has seemed impossible to climb. This valley has seemed unsurmountable, but I believe I am almost to the top of the mountain. I am filled with an inexpressible hope and wonder. What will it be like on the top of the mountain?

For I have come to turn "a man against his father, a daughter against her mother, a daughter-in-law against her mother-in-law—a man's enemies will be the members of his own household." Anyone who loves their father or mother more than me is not worthy of me; anyone who loves their son or daughter more than me is not worthy of me. Whoever does not take up their cross and follow me is not worthy of me.

Matthew 10:35–38

Then Nebuchadnezzar said, "Praise be to the God of Shadrach, Meshach, and Abednego, who has sent his angel and rescued his servants! They trusted in him and defied the king's command and were willing to give up their lives rather than serve or worship any god except their own God."

Daniel 3:28

"The light shines in the darkness, and the darkness has not overcome it" (John 1:5)

"In the shelter of your presence you hide them from all human intrigues; you keep them safe in your dwelling from accusing tongues" (Ps. 31:20).

"You will keep in perfect peace those whose minds are steadfast because they trust in you" (Isa. 26:3).

"For if you forgive other people when they sin against you, your heavenly Father will also forgive you" (Matt. 6:14).

"Because of the LORD's great love, we are not consumed, for his compassions never fail. They are new every morning; great is your faithfulness" (Lam. 3:22–23).

"And the peace of God, which transcends all understanding, will guard your hearts and your minds in Christ Jesus" (Phil. 4:7).

TWENTY-FIVE

October 19, 2017
Dear Jesus,

How many times have I prayed to You without hearing an answer? How many times have I prayed to You when it seemed like You were doing nothing? I am recalling times in my life where it seemed You were silent, unloving, uncaring, and far off. As a child I prayed for my parents to reconcile from their divorce, I prayed for healing from a health crisis, I prayed to keep babies, I prayed for deliverance from an unsafe situation, and I have prayed for reconciliation from broken relationships. My parents did not get back together, health answers have never arrived, I miscarried anyway, deliverance was almost longer than I could bear, and many broken relationships have not been restored. With this list, it looks like You do not care about me or have my best interest at heart, but I know You. I know from experience You are near, hear me, are faithful and love me.

From personal experience, I know that there is a whole picture I cannot see. I know Your ways are not my ways and Your ways are much higher than mine. I choose to trust You when I cannot see. God, help me believe this today when I cannot see the future. Help me recall all the wonderful things You have done for me in the past so I can rest knowing You will do the same for my future. Help me remember Your word as I wait to see my prayers answered. You care about me, have my best interest at heart, and You love me more than anyone else ever could. I may never see the whole picture, but I know that You do. Thank You for graciously revealing pieces of my whole picture as I love You and serve to love Your people.

"And this is my prayer: that your love may abound more and more in knowledge and depth of insight" (Phil. 1:9).

"Cast all your anxiety on him because he cares for you" (1 Peter 5:7).

"Many, LORD my God, are the wonders you have done, the things you planned for us. None can compare with you; were I to speak and tell of your deeds, they would be too many to declare" (Ps. 40:5).

"For God so loved the world that he gave his one and only Son, that whoever believes in him shall not perish but have eternal life" (John 3:16).

"The secret things belong to the LORD our God, but the things revealed belong to us and to our children forever, that we may follow all the words of this law" (Deut. 29:29).

"For we live by faith, not by sight" (2 Cor. 5:7).

TWENTY-SIX

November 27, 2017
Dear Jesus,

You will know the truth and the truth will set you free. (John 8:32) These sweet words play over and over in my mind. I have been waiting for this to be revealed in my life, but the truth is, it already has. I know the truth. You and I know the truth. I am free.

Why don't I feel free? Why do I feel the same? Still shackled by the lies. The hurts. Why when I am serving faithfully, do I still feel alone? Why when I am faithful to walk on the narrow path is there no reward in sight? Why when I am acting justly, am I still being slayed by hurtful words? Why when I sit quietly with You, Jesus, am I being scorned for not running the worldly race?

Thank You that You hear me and are near and faithful. Thank You that You never tire of my curiosity and my endless questions. Thank You that no weapon formed against me will prosper. I have peace because You know the truth, I know the truth, and I am free. You say that I am like a tree planted by streams of water, which yields its fruit in season and whose leaf does not wither. Whatever they do prospers. I want to believe this, but I just do not see it.

So, I have been wrestling with my thoughts which are unsettled by my outward feelings which are in direct conflict with Your word. If I am free, why do I feel forlorn? Shouldn't I be exuberant? If nothing in this world can harm me, shouldn't I be shouting with joy? If I am prospering and bearing fruit for the name of the Lord, shouldn't I be at peace? Today, it hit me straight in the heart. This is not about knowing the truth. I already know the truth. I am hung up on one thing. Justice. It just does not feel fair. To serve, to love, to trust and to still be persecuted. At one point in my life, I was sitting in a pew listening to a sermon on persecution and I heard the words, "In fact, everyone who wants to live a godly life in Christ Jesus will be persecuted" (2 Tim. 3:12). I remember thinking that I was not persecuted. Slowly, slowly did You begin to reveal persecution to me. It is becoming clearer. I was not made for this place. I am different. I am set apart. Just like You said, I am dying to self.

You gently reminded me in Your word today that justice is not my concern. You are a God who avenges. You are just and fair and will be the one to rule and judge the earth. Likewise, You will shape Your people how You see fit. On this journey here on earth, my job is to act justly, love mercy, and humbly walk with You. (Mic. 6:8) When I am obeying Your word, I am trusting in You. I am resting in truth. I am living freely. As I walk with, You, Jesus, I am secure. For You will go before me, and You will be my rear guard.

Here in this world it looks dismal, but I can shine radiantly because I am firmly planted in Your kingdom.

"No weapon formed against you will prosper" (Isa. 54:17).

"You are like a tree planted by streams of water, which yields its fruit in season and whose leaf does not wither—whatever they do prospers" (Ps. 1:3).

"The righteous will flourish like a palm tree, they will grow like a cedar of Lebanon; planted in the house of the Lord, they will flourish in the courts of our God" (Ps. 92:12–13).

"For the LORD will go before you, the God of Israel will be your rear guard" (Isa. 52:12).

"The LORD is a God who avenges. O God who avenges, shine forth. Rise up, Judge of the earth; pay back to the proud what they deserve" (Ps. 94:1–2).

TWENTY-SEVEN

December 14, 2017
Dear Jesus,

I feel as if I am being pummeled by waves. It seems as if anything and everything that could go wrong in my life has. I am serving, praying, worshipping and it feels as if my world is crashing in around me. I just had a car accident which infused a fight with Brandon, an unexpected illness is trying to take me out, another upsetting phone call from the school, appointment after appointment, hate mail, sibling fighting, another chipped tooth, another unwarranted text message, and the list goes on. My foot has slipped. I feel as if I am gasping for air, choking on water, crawling to shore after being shipwrecked for days. I am envisioning myself with my face in the sand, weeping and empty.

Where are You Jesus? I call out to You and I hear You say, "When you pass through the waters, I will be with you; and when you pass through the rivers, they will not sweep over you. When you walk through the fire, you will not be burned; the flames will not set you ablaze" (Isa. 43:2).

Help me. Please help me. Save me. Save my family. Protect us. Please God. The what if's and the why's are swallowing me whole. I hear You again, come. Come to the carpet. Palms up. Sit.

I do not want to come. I do not want to sit. I heard You, but instead of listening, I ran away from You, the only one who can fill my emptiness and hurting soul. I really do not want to go, but I hear You say, have another carpet ride and go and tell.

Fine.

I finally walked over to the carpet, sat crisscrossed and laid my palms on my knees face up. I am so empty. Fill me up with more of

You.

I heard You so clearly: stop being tossed back and forth. (Eph. 4:14) Greater is He who is in you than he who is in the world. (1 John 4:4) The battle is not yours, but mine. (2 Chr. 20:15) Keep your eyes on me.

I heard You, Jesus, loud and clear. As You spoke, Your peace swept over me. Forgive me yet again for trying to do everything in my own strength. I trust You. I will go up and write and tell of all the wonderful things You have done.

> "Listen, King Jehoshaphat and all who live in Judah and Jerusalem! This is what the LORD says to you: 'Do not be afraid or discouraged because of this vast army. For the battle is not yours, but God's.'"
>
> 2 Chronicles 20:15

"So, we fix our eyes not on what is seen, but on what is unseen, since what is seen is temporary, but what is unseen is eternal" (2 Cor. 4:18).

"Declare his glory among the nations, his marvelous deeds among all peoples" (Ps. 96:3).

TWENTY-EIGHT

January 22, 2018
Dear Jesus,

We are just getting back from Mexico. I love going on vacation and especially somewhere tropical. I loved having a new view, not just for my eyes, but for my mind. I needed time to take a step back so that I could move forward. I needed time for rest and respite. I needed time for awe. I sometimes miss awe and wonder at home. As I was taking in the new view, You revealed something new to me. A new wave of grief.

As I stepped off the plane, I took a deep breath in. I breathed out and captured a breathtaking view of the mountains caressed by endless waves. My breath shook as I breathed out. All the months of pent up anxiety and fear I blew out. I am afraid I have been living with a daily fear of an unwanted, unexpected visitor showing up on my doorstep. I was not crying on my trip or sad per say. I really had peace. I was enjoying the sunshine, laughter, and sounds of the waves. I was also enjoying the break from the everyday reality of dishes, laundry, and driving. I was loving the carefree time spent with Brandon and the kids where our biggest decision was lunch, swimming, an ice cream cone, or a Bahama Mama. While on the trip, every so often, something new emerged. Many feelings, thoughts, and unwanted memories of my past crept in my mind ever so subtly. On this trip the fear of being hurt at my house was removed and I entered a new wave of grief.

Jesus, grief is funny, unique, long-lasting, and surprising. I thought I was over my pain. I thought I had grieved all I could grieve, but this new wave of grief penetrated deep. I feel as if it went deep

103

into the next layer of my heart. Grief is such a lonely feeling. No one wants to hear about my pain any longer. I hear questions like why can't you let it go? Shouldn't you be over this by now? Why is it taking so long? Why can't you laugh it off? Why can't you brush it under the rug? Why can't you move on?

Thank You, Jesus, that when no one understands my pain You do and when everyone has had enough, You remain. God please help me heal. I do not want to be stuck in my pain. I want to move forward. Please help me do this. I know You have come to give me an abundant life. You have been good to me the whole time. I know You have been right here walking with me. Through reading and studying Your word, I have learned to apply many new things to my heart and as I am journaling to You, I feel peace enter. I know that You are powerful, sovereign, and all-knowing. I know that You love me, have a plan for my life and You will never leave me. Thank You for displaying Your glory in and through my life. I know I am not You and I do not have to know or understand what You are doing. Thank You for working through me and please sustain me as You work out Your will. I know there is a spiritual battle in the heavenly realm, but I know that I am not to fear because the enemy cannot touch me. Help me believe this when I am weak. Forgive me, God, for not fully trusting You and Your plan for my life. Forgive me for giving Satan more credit than he is due. Forgive me for bossing You around in my prayer life and thinking that I know best because the truth is, I know nothing, and You know everything.

Faith is coming into my life, and trust is entering my mind and I am learning to accept Your ways. You are mighty to save. I will be honest, Jesus, my life looks messy to me. My life looks broken in so many ways. All I can see is the brokenness and mess, but I believe from Your perspective it is all falling into place by Your divine hands. Help me see this.

"And the peace of God, which transcends all understanding, will guard your hearts and your minds in Christ Jesus" (Phil. 4:7).

"For whenever our heart condemns us, God is greater than our heart, and he knows everything" (1 John 3:20).

"For God so loved the world that he gave his one and only Son, that whoever believes in him shall not perish but have eternal life" (John 3:16).

"Heal me, LORD, and I will be healed; save me and I will be saved, for you are the one I praise" (Jer. 17:14).

"Cast all your anxiety on him because he cares for you" (1 Pet. 5:7).

"'For my thoughts are not your thoughts, neither are your ways my ways,' declares the LORD" (Isa. 55:8).

TWENTY-NINE

March 1, 2018
Dear Jesus,

Approximately eleven years ago, I sat in a room with a group of women. I did not know these women well at all. I was uncomfortable with this unfamiliar situation. I received an email a few days prior inviting me to a Bible study. I thought I was invited by mistake, but curiosity got the best of me and I went afraid. This was my first Bible study and here Your word came alive to me. It was when I heard You speak to me for the first time. On the page in front of me I read, "Draw near to God and he will draw near to you" (James 4:8). I remember being filled with amazement realizing that You do talk back to Your children. As a child I prayed to You many, many times. So many prayers had gone up, but I never heard a response. Jesus, I will never forget the first time I heard You speak to me.

As a newly surrendered Christian, I found myself with a burning desire for everyone I knew to know You and Your amazing love. I was so full of passion, but I was unable to express it in words. I was devouring Your word, but I could not explain what I was learning, and this was so frustrating to me. To me, Your message was so simple and yet I could not tell anyone about You in a clear, concise way. This desire to share was not just for my family and friends, but for a hurting world who desperately needed Your truth. I know now this desire in me was not me, but Your Spirit in me.

Many years have passed since this first Bible study and I have slowly learned to share You and my faith with family, friends, and others. Over the last couple of years, I have lost many people in my life including family members, old and new friends, and people I love dearly. I wondered, Jesus, why You would allow these relationships to dissolve after I had worked so hard building these relationships so that I could share my faith and see these loved ones turn to You. I am starting to see the problem. I am the problem. I forget that I am not doing the work. You are the one who is doing the work, the one with the plan and the purpose. Help me remember there is a time for everything, and my only job is to love, obey and walk with You. I have been holding on so tight, gripping everything within reach, clinging to anyone and everything, carrying so many burdens that are so heavy for me. Why do I think I have to carry any and everyone's faith including my own? Help me cast my cares on You Lord and drop off all the baggage I carry that is not mine to carry. I only want to be Your vessel.

Relationships are complicated, God. You have been teaching me a difficult lesson about the pearls You have entrusted to me. Now I know that not everyone can cherish my pearls. Help me love people and show Your love without giving them what is sacred. The truth is many people are not ready for my pearls and they cannot handle them, and they certainly do not know what to do with them. Help me choose friends carefully and help me remember not everyone is my best friend. Help me be kind, full of Your love, but also full of Your wisdom. Help me remember not everyone is who they seem to be and not everyone's motives and hearts are pure. Help me identify whose hearts are truly toward You and the ones who look like You and sound like You, but are far from You, Jesus. Help me remember that it is okay to distance myself gracefully from people who are not honorable, consistent, and not committed to growing.

Thank You for blessing me beyond measure. You have given me a jewelry box full of beautiful pearls that I cherish. You have given me so much, but I know everyone who has been given much, much more will be demanded and the one who has been entrusted with much, much more will be asked. I hear You asking me to humbly walk with

You, to be separate, to lose people for the sake of truth, to seek what is eternal not temporary, to share when it is uncomfortable, to wait indefinitely, and to trust when I cannot see. The only way I can do this is by Your wisdom and help. Not by might or power, but by Your Spirit. (Zech. 4:6) Thank You for equipping me.

"Do not give dogs what is sacred; do not throw your pearls to pigs. If you do, they may trample them under their feet, and turn and tear you to pieces" (Matt. 7:6).

"He has shown you, O mortal, what is good. And what does the LORD require of you? To act justly and to love mercy and to walk humbly with your God" (Mic. 6:8).

"From everyone who has been given much, much will be demanded; and from the one who has been entrusted with much, much more will be asked" (Luke 12:48).

THIRTY

March 13, 2018
Dear Jesus,

Last week was a terrible week. My brand-new washing machine still is not running properly as it continues to foam over day after day, week after week. Relationships in my life continue to get messier and messier. Sickness has entered my house and my life has been filled with appointment after appointment. My computer crashed for the third time in a year and a half not to mention it is tax season and we are self-employed. Strangely enough I was calm, did what I had to do, pressed forward, and took time to pray through every mishap and misfortune. I just kept taking the next best step and I did not become unraveled or upset until I did.

I wept, loudly and ugly. As I sobbed, I did the unthinkable. I questioned Your goodness with all my whys. Why, Lord, after I gave my life to You is everything so hard? Why do I have one problem after another? Why after I obey You time and time again do You allow more hardship? Why have I lost another person I love? Why is my marriage struggling? Why are my children misbehaving? Do You not love me? Is this Christian walk worth it? Haven't I done everything You have asked of me? Why? Why? Why? And then came the conviction, what have I done? Oh, Jesus, forgive me.

I was studying Your word this morning and a verse jumped off the screen at me. "For you know the grace of our Lord Jesus Christ, that though he was rich, yet for your sake he became poor, so that you through his poverty might become rich" (2 Cor. 8:9). Forgive me for my selfishness. You do not owe me anything. You died for me, period. Tears of thankfulness slid down my cheeks. Thank You for not leaving me in this selfish state of woe is me. Everything I do for You is not to get credit or for a more blessed life. I do it all because of love. My love for You and Your love for me. As my week ended and my life continued Your blessings began to peek through by answering my prayers in unexplainable ways. One thing I keep hearing is I am free. I am no longer in bondage to this temporal life. Thank You for making me for eternity and giving me an eternal inheritance. Help me keep my eyes on You not on what is seen.

My Christian life. Hope. Trust. Love. My lows are low, and they have gone much lower than I would like them to go, but oh the highs. The highs are so much higher. I am soaring on the heights, I can scale a wall, I can walk on water all because I am not alone. You are leading me to places I could have never gone on my own. Thank You.

"Set your minds on things above, not on earthly things" (Col. 3:2).

"With your help I can advance against a troop; with my God I can scale a wall" (Ps. 18:29).

THIRTY-ONE

March 16, 2018
Dear Jesus,

I was sitting in church on Sunday and I loved the message, the music, the movie clip, and the preaching. I could feel the Spirit moving until I was suddenly distracted. I was watching everyone sitting in my row, the row in front of me, and on every side of me. My mind was on any and everything except the message. My mind was chaotic, judgmental, and full of unrest. Communion commenced and the band began to play a song. I took a piece of bread as I felt the distraction in my mind dissipate. I looked up, closed my eyes, and heard You whisper, "Look at me, stop judging others, just love them."

Why is this so hard? Why am I so caught up in trying to make others behave just like me? Why do I think I know what is best for other people? Why do I judge their every move, their faith, their motives, and their heart? Thank You for stopping me in my tracks. Thank You for reminding me I cannot change people and it is not my job. Thank You for reminding me that what I can do is extend grace. I know this is what You lavish on me daily. Help me look past the muck and mire and love people. I want to wrap my arm around a loved one, hold a hand, crack a knuckle, twirl some hair, and smile. When I hear a grumble in the morning instead of grumbling back, I want to choose grace. When someone snaps a harsh word or a reckless text, I want to choose grace. When someone shrugs their shoulder, rolls their eyes, or walks away from me, I want to choose grace. Jesus, help me look beyond my feelings, and hurts to bless with the ultimate gift, grace.

Help me remember the difference between the law and the new

113

covenant. Remind me daily that at one time I could never measure up or be good enough, but now I do not have to be. Thank You for dying on the cross in my place paying the ultimate penalty to extend grace to me and cleaning me from all my unrighteousness. Help me extend this grace to all the people around me.

> For it is by grace you have been saved, through faith—and this is not from yourselves, it is the gift of God—not by works, so that no one can boast. For we are God's handiwork, created in Christ Jesus to do good works, which God prepared in advance for us to do.
>
> Ephesians 2:8–10

"But God demonstrates his own love for us in this: While we were still sinners, Christ died for us" (Rom. 5:8).

"For all have sinned and fall short of the glory of God" (Rom. 3:23).

"He lifted me out of the slimy pit, out of the mud and mire; he set my feet on a rock and gave me a firm place to stand" (Ps. 40:2).

"See what great love the Father has lavished on us, that we should be called children of God! And that is what we are! The reason the world does not know us is that it did not know him" (1 John 3:1).

"There is only one Lawgiver and Judge, the one who is able to save and destroy. But you—who are you to judge your neighbor?" (James 4:12).

THIRTY-TWO

April 16, 2018
Dear Jesus,

You have been busy here. I see You at work in my life and the lives of people around me. I am capturing beautiful views of Your story and I am humbled to be used in Your plans for Your kingdom and glory. The last couple weeks have been terribly busy and You have put on my heart many opportunities to serve Your people. These opportunities have been endless and have taken me out of my comfort zone. I have been stretched to extend comfort when it was hard for me to walk through and witness the pain. It would be so easy to just feel sad for the families and do nothing more than think of them, or pray, or quickly attend services or visitations. No, I hear You telling me to show up on the doorstep, walk through the line, and meet a sad loved one face-to-face. It is hard to get dirty and feel the pain that affects others. I have realized that getting dirty and allowing feelings to surface is so healing and liberating. Bringing the mess into the light allows it to be seen, felt, and healed by You. I have been blessed in all the ways I have served in the last couple of weeks. You have brought me such a rare joy in the serving. A joy that bubbled over the surface, spilled across my face and into my actions. I was serving to bless others, but in return I was the one blessed beyond measure.

When I heard You say "Go," I went filled with trepidation to wherever You were calling me. As I served, I saw You show up in some of the most unexpected places confirming to me I was in the right place at the right time on the narrow road You prepared for me. New relationships were made, there was joy mingled with sadness, there was new life made where there was death. Every situation was directed by Your hand and intricately woven into my life and the lives of others. You are a detail-oriented Father. I stand in awe of Your ways. There is no one like You.

"Do nothing out of selfish ambition or vain conceit. Rather, in humility value others above yourselves" (Phil. 2:3).

"Give, and it will be given to you. A good measure, pressed down, shaken together, and running over, will be poured into your lap. For with the measure you use, it will be measured to you" (Luke 6:38).

"Indeed, the very hairs of your head are all numbered" (Luke 12:7).

"Each of you should use whatever gift you have received to serve others, as faithful stewards of God's grace in its various forms" (1 Pet. 4:10).

"For we are God's handiwork, created in Christ Jesus to do good works, which God prepared in advance for us to do" (Eph. 2:10).

"No one is like you, LORD; you are great, and your name is mighty in power" (Jer. 10:6).

"Therefore, my dear friends, as you have always obeyed—not only in my presence, but now much more in my absence—continue to work out your salvation with fear and trembling" (Phil. 2:12).

THIRTY-THREE

April 16, 2018
Dear Jesus,

It seems my life is like a cycle. I have experienced coasting, growing, and stretching periods. When I am smack dab in the thick of a personal season of stretching, I cannot see what is happening; however, when I come full circle, I can look back and see Your footprint and divine purpose in my pain. The past couple of years have been a stretching period for me and I feel as I have been stripped clean or mangled, whatever You want to call it. I believe You would say it better. "I will refine them like silver and test them like gold" (Zech. 13:9). Yes, Jesus, I have been refined. Through the refinement I have called on Your name and You have answered me. I am Yours and You are mine.

Jesus, a little while ago You brought someone new into my life. Someone I knew, but not well. As we began to get to know each other, I believe I stepped on her toes. Judging our past experiences, I opened my mouth and shared, in a casual group setting where my new friend was presently. I am incredibly careful with my words and I believed I was in this situation as well, but my friend startled me with harsh, possibly true words. I was uncomfortable with an uneasy feeling in the pit of my stomach the rest of the time we gathered. Was this conviction? Most of my afternoon was spent dwelling on the conversation and I went over my words a hundred times, sought wise counsel, prayed collectively and alone. The feeling persisted and I drafted an email and sent it to my new friend. What came after the email was a gift. A gift of peace, friendship, and a gift the enemy did not want opened.

Our friendship began on rocky ground; however, settled on a firm foundation, You, Jesus. We do life together, pour into each other life-breathing words, help, care for, and love one another. I believe You orchestrated this relationship for such a time as this. It became noticeably clear to me when my friend began a new trial that would have been hard to navigate without me. To my surprise, the trial was remarkably like the one I have been walking for a while. You knew my friend would have to walk this path and in love and care for her You provided me, someone who could relate to her pain and say, "Me too, this is hard and I am here." You provided simple me, someone who had been comforted by You. Full circle.

I wonder how many times this happens. How many times do I miss the gifts You prepare for me? Immediately after You showed me how You were working in my life in this situation You graciously showed me more. Why am I surprised? You are a good, good Father.

It came in the form of a text message. Someone special to me reached out hurting from a harsh conversation which was laced in judgement and poor timing. This conversation allowed doubt to creep in and lies to take hold and was led by a believer. Instead of loving there was judging, instead of grace there was guilt and instead of forgiveness there was condemnation. Strangely enough it was a situation I had just been through, wrestled with for years, and begged You for answers. In my situation I desperately wanted You to show me Your truth, and clarity. You comforted me with all compassion revealing truth through Your written word and faithfully answering all my nagging questions filling me with love, grace, and forgiveness. I was able to respond to my hurting loved one. I poured out my heart with truth. Everything I had learned and searched so hard for came flowing out in love, grace and forgiveness pointing him straight to You, not religion. I stomped out the judgement, guilt, and condemnation before they were able to take root and set up shop. Full circle.

Both situations could have gone in a different direction had

I not been in Your word and prayer. If I had not been in constant relationship with You, I could have taken a different path where I would have missed out on building a beautiful relationship because of pride. Or I may have missed the opportunity to minister to a friend in need or missed out on all the wisdom she witnessed to me in my time of need. Or I may have missed out in the privilege of showing someone You and Your truth. I may have missed being a part of Your divine nature to comfort those in any trouble with the comfort we ourselves receive from You. Ultimately, I may have missed the joy in watching Your story unfold.

Oh, how I love You and Your ways. I love seeing Your work unfold. Oh, how I am humbled to be a part of Your plan and watch Your glory displayed. It is worth it to endure pain for Your purpose, to love others, point them to You, and ultimately join the church in glorifying the Father.

> Praise be to the God and Father of our Lord Jesus Christ, the Father of compassion and the God of all comfort, who comforts us in all our troubles, so that we can comfort those in any trouble with the comfort we ourselves receive from God.
>
> 2 Corinthians 1:3–4

> For if you remain silent at this time, relief and deliverance for the Jews will arise from another place, but you and your father's family will perish. And who knows but that you have come to your royal position for such a time as this?"
>
> Esther 4:14

THIRTY-FOUR

April 30, 2018
Dear Jesus,

My fear is real, paralyzing and debilitating. Fear has plagued the last two years of my life. My home should be a safe place secured by Your sacred boundary; however, fear has snuck in and I have let fear overrule my faith and I have entered the realm of the unknown. Questions fill my mind in a chaotic splatter filling up the spaces in my brain. Who is this person now? What will they do to me and my family? At what length will they go to protect their image? Who will believe me? Who will help me? Where I once felt safe, I now feel scared. Where I once ran to, I now run from. Where I once trusted, I now doubt. Fear entered in the form of text messages, emails, hate-mail, and phone calls incessantly interrupting my life. The fear has been unescapable filled with lies, hate, and manipulation. I loathe how darkness has snuck into my mind and life stealing my love, peace, and joy.

Instead of running to You and Your word I relied on myself franticly preparing boundaries. I blocked messages, emails, mail delivery, and my phone from the hatred and peace washed over me until, it appeared. There was an illegal trespass and I panicked, my heart raced, my breaths heaved, and the thought emerged, *I will never be safe.*

Thank You as I turned my gaze to You and sought You, You answered me and delivered me from all my fears. I know by reading Your word I am not to fear, but I have learned it is a natural part of life. It is a feeling and as I am living here on earth in my flesh, I feel fear. In my situation my fear is real because there is a risk for me, my family, and my personal belongings; however, I have learned it is what I do with my fear that really matters. I am choosing to run straight to Your arms. You are my refuge, my ever-present help in trouble, You hear me, and I am never alone. I know that You can handle all of me, the good, the bad and the ugly. Thank You, Jesus, that I can pour everything on You straight from my heart and You carry it and do what only You can do, protect me.

Forgive me for believing all the lies and letting fear replace my faith. My fear was too big, and it blocked the truth for a minute, but thankfully Your light shines in the darkness and the darkness cannot overcome it. Your word has become a beacon of light expelling lies and revealing truth. I am so grateful I know the truth and the truth has set me free. Thank You for hemming me in behind and before and laying Your hand on me. You keep me, Jesus. Thank You that I do not have to fear anything that comes near me day or night because of You it will not come near me. Thank You, Jesus, for commanding Your angels concerning me and guarding me in all Your ways. My eyes are on You and Your eternal promise. You are a hearer and deliverer and because of You I am radiant and never covered with shame. Fear, but God. You are beautiful and powerful and there is no one like You. Thank You for speaking to me originally and touching me in the center of my heart. Because of You, fear dissolved in Your presence. I will praise You because I know the truth now, and I am always safe.

"I sought the LORD, and he answered me; he delivered me from all my fears. Those who look to him are radiant; their faces are never covered with shame" (Ps. 34:4–5).

"God is our refuge and strength, an ever-present help in trouble" (Ps. 46:1).

"Have I not commanded you? Be strong and courageous. Do not be afraid; do not be discouraged, for the LORD your God will be with you wherever you go" (Josh. 1:9).

"For we live by faith, not by sight" (2 Cor. 5:7).

"The thief comes only to steal and kill and destroy; I have come that they may have life and have it to the full" (John 10:10).

"The light shines in the darkness, and the darkness has not overcome it" (John 1:5).

"You hem me in behind and before, and you lay your hand upon me" (Ps. 139:5).

> You will not fear the terror of night, nor the arrow that flies by day, nor the pestilence that stalks in the darkness, nor the plague that destroys at midday. A thousand may fall at your side, ten thousand at your right hand, but it will not come near you. For he will command his angels concerning you to guard you in all your ways.
>
> Psalm 91:5–7, 11

THIRTY-FIVE

May 7, 2018
Dear Jesus,

There is only one You. On August 17, 2008, I read the words, "For I know the plans I have for you, declares the Lord, plans to prosper you and not to harm you, plans to give you a hope and a future" (Jer. 29:11) as I was baptized. I loved and found comfort in Your special words. I know these words were not written to me; however, I know they were written for me. I had no idea at the time that I read them how powerful these words would be. As Your new follower, I had no idea where I was going or what plans You had for me and I remember asking You many times what Your special plans were. I finally tired of asking and I scribbled the question on a scratch piece of paper, and I tucked it neatly in to the pages of the worn Bible I was given as a child. I trusted You to show me in time.

It has been almost ten years and many trials since I read those words in front of a full congregation. Much pain and suffering has occurred since I declared my love and devotion to You. Satan intended to harm me through many events, but You took what he meant for harm and turned it for my good. Something new began to emerge through my grieving. Endless days of crying and anguish could not be contained any longer and it started spilling onto the pages of scratch paper, journals, my phone and eventually advanced to the surface of my computer. Writing became a way for me to process my pain. In time, I began sharing my story and writing with others in hopes that others would be enlightened to Your goodness. Over the course of a year and a half, many people began asking me if I had thought of publishing my writings. What do You think, Jesus? If this is Your desire for me, would

You open the door when the time is right?

An opportunity arrived in my inbox inviting me to a special event. I felt that it was from You and I was exhilarated and excited to participate more than anything. Many confirmations came, much spiritual resistance occurred, and much prayer went up, and in the end, I took a leap and registered to participate, trusting You as my guide. Many decisions had to be made regarding the conference and every step of the way I sought Your face. Your special words "For I know the plans I have for you" continue to pop up in messages, phone calls, devotionals, and cards. Oh, how sweet the sound of Your special words filling me to overflowing, but then I wonder, my writings Lord? Are these the special plans for me? Is this how You will use me?

I am starting to take risks and make bold moves knowing that You are with me. Every time I make a move, a spiritual attack happens and my mind wages war on me. Questions flood my mind... why did you do that? What will people think? You are not qualified to write. You are not equipped to do this. But God. You enter my thoughts and whisper, "When you are weak, then you are strong." Just as Abraham did, I am choosing to follow You even when I do not know where I am going. I am encouraged by other believers and their timely messages they are sending me. They are giving me the courage I need to press forward in truth and boldness. I am trusting that in my weaknesses You will prove strong and have the victory advancing Your kingdom despite my inadequacy. This road of being courageous is hard and it is proving to be difficult and though some may be afraid to walk it, I am not going to be that person.

Only You could work what Satan meant to harm me and turn it for my good. Through adversity I am growing and blessing others through Your strength. You cause awe and wonder to fill my entire being. Sometimes I feel as though I might explode into glory. I am overwhelmed by Your nearness, faithfulness, and gracious mercy. There is no love like Yours. No one can thwart Your plan and Your purpose will always prevail. This is my story for Your glory.

"That is why, for Christ's sake, I delight in weaknesses, in insults, in hardships, in persecutions, in difficulties. For when I am weak, then I am strong" (2 Cor. 12:10).

"For the revelation awaits an appointed time; it speaks of the end and will not prove false. Though it lingers, wait for it; it will certainly come and will not delay" (Hab. 2:3).

"Many are the plans in a person's heart, but it is the LORD's purpose that prevails" (Prov. 19:21).

"Being confident of this, that he who began a good work in you will carry it on to completion until the day of Christ Jesus" (Phil. 1:6).

THIRTY-SIX

May 25, 2018
Dear Jesus,

Send. It is just a little four-letter word, but, oh, the power. This word creates so many feelings inside of me. Over the last decade, I have been finding my way on Your path. I know You grant everyone special gifts to be used for Your glory. For me, it has taken many prayers, questions, and thoughts to realize Your desire for me. I believe gifts are unique and tailored especially for us and the circle of people You place around us. You have placed on my heart a passionate desire to encourage others with Your word. It sounds beautiful, seems wonderful, and it is, but it is also hard. You repeatedly ask me to do hard and uncomfortable things. You ask me to put others ahead of my needs, to step into hard places to comfort others in need, ask me to stand on truth, to be separate and to stand alone if need be. You ask me to send verses, cards, books, flowers, cookies, emails, and letters. How can I do this, Jesus?

Send. What a word. Jesus, this word is hard for me to obey. It sounds kind, nice, and loving and it is those things, but it is also full of other things. To follow through on it takes attributes I do not naturally possess. It takes someone brave, courageous, bold, thick-skinned, independent, and confident. You must be up there on Your throne just laughing at me, not in a mean way, but in a way that says I will do immeasurably more than you ask or imagine. I am not brave and courageous or bold and thick-skinned or independent and confident. Hitting that four-letter word on my computer is hard for me. I like people and I want them to like me. I do care about what they think of me, maybe way too much. Jesus, being set apart takes guts and to be honest, I do not have it, not even a little bit. I have always been the girl who wanted to fit in and did what it took to be in the popular crowd. My natural tendencies are to fit in, lie, hide, and quit when things get tough, not stick my nose out or stand out and up for truth. The unknown is the killer for me. I wonder, how will they receive me? What will they think of me? Will Your word be offensive to them? Will they look at me differently? Will this affect my family? Will I look weird? Then I heard You. *I chose the foolish things of the world to shame the wise; I chose the weak things of the world to shame the strong. I chose the lowly things of this world and the despised things, and the things that are not, to nullify the things that are so that no one can boast. I am Your wisdom, righteousness, holiness, and redemption.*

I hear You, Lord. You use broken, foolish, weak, lowly, and the worst things. You chose me just the way I am. You love the questioning, over-thinking, deep-feeling, thin-skinned, uncertain, doubtful me. I know that my gifts, my story, and my writings are not mine, but Yours. You have tailor made me for the King. I know I cannot do anything in my own strength, and You are the one who is equipping me to do Your will.

Honestly, Jesus, I do not know what people think when they receive encouragement from me. My mind has plenty of scenarios, but I hope what they do see is Your love. Help me do the things You want me to do regardless of hearing a response or not. Jesus, help me care more about what You think of me than anyone else. Help me continue with the work You prepared for me willingly. Help me be brave and obey You when You say send or go.

I just sent my hardest send so far. I submitted a transparent, personal writing I felt unqualified and unequipped to send. I had so much fear and trembling, but I did it anyway because I believed You wanted me to do it and I believed You would confirm it to me by sending a blessing for obeying. I really wanted my writing to affect and overwhelm the readers in the center of their heart, and I had hope until my expectations were dashed. I am not going to lie, Jesus, I was disappointed. I did not believe I should have a chance, but God. My thoughts allowed a foothold from the enemy and I sunk in my thoughts. I am so weak, and these thoughts ruled my mind. Thoughts like, why did I do that? I am not a writer. I am not good enough. What did you think people would think? Why did you put yourself out there for people to see? Then Your truth appeared, and I began to look at all the things that did happen because of this submission. Trust reappeared and I am boldly proclaiming, "I did it because You said so. Period."

My path is dimly lit, and I can only see the next step in front of me. I do not know why You are asking me to encourage others, write, or continue to send, but I know You have a plan and Your plans are good. I will believe when I cannot see and obey Your call knowing that when I am weak, I am strong.

"Each of you should use whatever gift you have received to serve others, as faithful stewards of God's grace in its various forms" (1 Pet. 4:10).

"Therefore, my dear friends, as you have always obeyed—not only in my presence, but now much more in my absence—continue to work out your salvation with fear and trembling" (Phil. 2:12).

"For we live by faith, not by sight" (2 Corinthians 5:7).

THIRTY-SEVEN

July 12, 2018
Dear Jesus,

I just plopped down in my chair between two of my girlfriends as we got ready to watch a little baseball. We began what we do best, talk. We talked about our struggles, our highs, and everything in between until it came to an abrupt halt. I heard, "Mom!" I whipped my head around to see one of my sons racing toward me. He mouthed, breathless, a word I would like to take back. "Ella."

I remember yelling, "Is she okay?" I will never forget the look on his face, the panic in his eyes and the no written in the shake of his head. I began running toward him, the playground behind him and my sweet Ella. And that is when I saw her lying motionless below the play equipment. I crouched down next to her as she was gasping for air. I dialed our doctor's office across the street which had just closed within two minutes of the call. Panicked I turned around and yelled to my friend, "Get a nurse!" Ella could not breathe. I kept whispering, "Breathe, breathe, breathe, Baby." In those few seconds, I realized I had to call 911. Beyond whispering Your name to Ella, I do not remember much of the event. The last thing I remember is tossing my keys to one of my boys as I stepped into the ambulance.

Silence ensued as Ella's breathing began to go back to normal. I remember looking out the window as we drove down the street. Everything felt so surreal. Life was going on around me, but I did not feel normal at all. I watched as my husband's work truck passed us heading toward the park to pick up my vehicle. I felt numb inside and then I heard it so clearly, "Kari, you have no control. Let it all go. I am the One who controls all things. Be still and know that I am God (Ps. 46:10)." At this moment I knew it. I had no control of anything, not even the safety and protection of my sweet baby girl. In one second, my life could have been changed forever and I could not have done one thing to stop it.

At the start of this day, I believed I was not the controlling girl I once was. I had relinquished control of trying to change my husband, my children, my life, and my circumstances. My new personality went with the flow, rolled with the punches of this life, and cared more about others than controlling the time and sequence of events. Or so I thought. In this quiet place in the ambulance I realized I still believed I had some control. I believed I could keep my kids safe and protected. I was wrong. Accidents happen. Life happens. God is the one who is there to protect, love, and carry us through any circumstance.

In the emergency room, Ella was strapped flat on a board with a neck brace on. She was shaken up and so was I. I was desperately trying to hold in my tears. I did well until Brandon appeared. I am sure he could read every emotion spread across my face and then the tears fell from Ella's eyes. I whispered gently in her ear love and compassion for the traumatic event that had just taken place. Brandon moved close and did the same as we gently began to remove all the wood chips that were tucked in every nook and cranny. The doctor came in and slowly examined Ella. Miraculously, she had no signs of a concussion. She was practically scratch free. The doctor went down one vertebra at a time and Ella felt no pain. Slowly Ella sat up and then moved to a standing position. The only thing she could not do was bend over. X-rays were taken, and no evidence of fracture was seen. She was almost perfect. I will take "just sore" over every other possibility that I had thought of.

How? How was she perfect? Scratch free? Fine? The morning after the accident I was helping Ella in the bathroom. I was brushing her hair and I had asked her if she remembered me whispering Your name to her while we were waiting for the ambulance. She nodded. I told my sweet girl that You were with her. She said frankly, "Mom, Jesus is always with me. He's with me right now."

Weeks later we were back at the same park and Brandon went over with Ella, so she could show him what happened. We were shocked to learn Ella fell much further than the five or six feet we originally thought. Ella fell nine feet flat on her back. She had nothing to show she had fallen, not even one scratch. How? The only answer I can come up with was You had Your hand on her. You were protecting, loving, and carrying her and then You did the same for me riding in the ambulance. In the quietness I heard You, be still and know that I am God.

THIRTY-EIGHT

July 18, 2018
Dear Jesus,

It is dark. I hear snoring and see the soft light of the moon peering through my window. The covers are soft and warmth envelops me. I begin to lift my head to roll over and searing pain shoots up my neck. It happened again. I cannot move. This is how my week began. Pain and minimal movement were my reality. The medication regimen began as well as the chiropractic appointments. The smell of Bengay and I were interchangeable. Life as a mother of four does not stop when ailments occur. Life continued at a breakneck pace. Simultaneously text messages began to flood my phone. My friend traveling to St. Paul, Minnesota, for the Christian Writing Conference was most likely not going to be able to go. My palms turn from warm to clammy in seconds. Thoughts began to take over me. Should I still go alone? What will my husband say? How will I do this? Maybe I should not go.

The week moved swiftly. I began preparation for the writing conference. As coffee filled the air, I slowly poured my first cup. Eyes still half open as warmth filled my mouth. My feet lazily hit one step at a time as I gradually made my way to the computer where plumbing invoices plead for my attention. Moments later as I began my work, I clicked my accounting program. Nothing. Again. Nothing.

Hot sticky air hit my face as I stepped in my car. Frustration bubbled under the surface and anxiety simmered on top and pain pressed into every movement. Seriousness etched the curves of my face as we entered the restaurant. We greeted my mom with a smile as we pressed into the squishy booth seats that we loved. Chips and salsa were placed in the center of the table as we all dug in. Conversation began and took an unexpected turn. "Can we go through Verona on our way home?" asked one of my children.

"No," I said puzzled. I needed to get home to fix our accounting program before I headed out of town in the morning.

"I thought we were going to pick up my iPhone 6," my son stated boldly.

Bewilderment entered my expression as I said, "Not today, son." Something was going on. Why did he think he was getting a phone today? Where did this thought come from? Why was this all happening before I left on my trip?

Lunch continued with dirty looks, heavy sighing, arms, and elbows sprawled on the table in between all the dishes and silverware. I ate silently. The seriousness etched on the curves of my face turned to deeply creased lines on my flesh. As I pushed through the door of the restaurant moist, hot air hit my face. I took a heavy breath as I entered my car. My mom waved goodbye with a hesitant look spread across her face. I laid my head on the hard, gray steering wheel and wept. Jesus, prove it. Prove You want me to go.

My head hung as I climbed the stairs to my computer and the lingering dilemma. As I began to work, my disgruntled son continued to nag me from the navy blue sofa in our office. I began softly humming a hymn and he calmly moseyed over and began to rub my arm. He then crossed the plush, gray carpet back to the couch, laid his head down and slept.

After hours of work, the computer complication was resolved, and these thoughts emerged. Tomorrow. Tomorrow is the day I leave. Broken. Alone. Afraid. Should I go? As the thoughts left, I stood up from my computer. The soft carpet was filled with scattered papers and frayed edges of loose-leaf papers Brandon left behind. He loves to see his progress by how large his piles are. He likes me to see them too. I smiled as I knelt to gather the hard work into piles. A piece of red on a post card from a flyer in a newspaper peeked out from underneath the mountain of papers. I gently pulled it out and in astonishment I laid my head into my hands as I praised You. Yes, Lord. I will follow You anywhere You ask me to go. Your personal message resonated in the center of my heart.

The whirring of the blow dryer was in the background as my son entered the bathroom. I set the big yellow blow dryer on the brown granite counter. I began to finish tracing my eyes with my Barely Black Liner as the soft white curtain with yellow flowers lining my shower slinked closed.

"Mom?"

"Yeah."

"You know what I was thinking about yesterday at lunch with grandma?"

"No," I said when I wanted to say, I do not know maybe an iPhone 6 with a silver case. My mouth remained sealed after "no" left my lips.

"I was thinking that God is testing you."

"M-hmmm," the sound left my lips, but my jaw hit the floor.

"First your back and you can't turn your head. Now your friend can't go with you and you have to go alone."

"Hmmm."

"Mom?"

"Yeah?"

"I think you are brave."

"I love you, son."

I set my pencil down and wiped tears streaking down my cheeks. You are whispering to my son. My children are watching my walk with You. He thinks I am brave. This is not what I thought was happening at the lunch table.

My car pulled out of our long gravel driveway. Dust billowed up around the car as a cardinal flew in front of the windshield. I breathed in the cool air from the air-conditioned vent. I am doing this.

The drive was easy. It was quiet in the car. I listened to music and talked with You as I drove. When I greeted the city, I recognized my love for the country. Sweat began to roll down my back. My mouth was dry, and my face was pinched. Directions were flying off my GPS faster than I could read them. Flashing lights, lane changes and, I am not going to lie, there was some honking...at me. I took an extra, unexpected lap to my hotel. As my pearly white SUV slid in between two yellow painted lines. I breathed.

I entered a gray hotel with concrete walls. I checked in and walked with my plastic key pinched between my fingers as I pushed the up button next to the beige, scratched elevator. I pushed through the door and cold air punched my face. I dropped all my baggage off my shoulders as it ripped my skin sliding down hitting the floor. I crumpled onto the bed. I was greeted by more utter silence.

I gathered more courage and began to navigate my way through the streets of Minnesota. Moments later, my car pulled onto a long, paved road surrounded by trees and lush gardens. The road was lined with beautiful brick buildings and I heard water in the distance. As I walked along a clean, wide sidewalk toward the building where the registration table was, I saw a beautiful fountain with benches around it. I grabbed the handle of the glass door with my wet palm.

This is what these two days were like. Silence and nervousness followed by more silence and more nervousness. I was uncomfortable. Plain and simple.

Both keynote speakers left me longing for more of You, Jesus. When these women spoke, You could tell they had been with You. I cherished their words and their ability to allow You to make beauty from their ashes. Two things left an imprint on my heart. First, my scars are my authority which defeats the enemy reminding me fears are just a lie. Second, I am not just called to be a steward with what God has financially blessed me with. I am called to be a steward with all things He blesses on my path including my pain.

Time was moving quickly. My one-on-one appointment was

rapidly approaching. I was nervous as I sat down at the panel luncheon table. I was uncomfortable as I took my seat. Panic crept back in. My gum. No garbage. No paper napkins. No familiar face. I did something I have not done since elementary school. Something ridiculous. I swallowed my gum there in a room filled with beautiful, educated writers. After flipping my lettuce with my fork for the hundredth time, I excused myself early for my highly anticipated one-on-one meeting. Words played over and over in my mind. Nervous joy swept across my face as I fiddled with my binder. My cherished binder. She was going to read my writings. This was too exciting to contain. When the bell rang the one-minute warning I stood, gathered my black-and-white bag containing my precious two years of hard work and straightened my dress. The bell rang for the last time. I stepped forward.

Ten minutes later I walked away with my head down and my feet sliding in my black wedge sandals. A tear was begging to drop as I hurriedly went down the white tile steps straight to the door. What the heck just happened?

The rest of the afternoon was inconsequential. I moved from room to room distracted. I resisted note taking and evaded the lessons. An hour early, I lifted my head high and pushed through the glass door for the last time. I walked down the pristine walkway, passed the water fountain and beyond the last brick building. I crossed the filled stalls until I came across my car. I placed my bag in the trunk and slinked in between the door and the charcoal gray console. What the heck was that? What? What? Why did You send me? What do You want me to do with this? Why did I uproot my life for this? What? I drove down the long, paved road toward the city.

My what questions continued as sweat reappeared all over my body traveling from one interchange to the next. As I distanced myself from the city my breathing returned to steady and my sweating stopped leaving only my damp clothes behind. Silence commenced, and I wrestled in my mind with all my longing questions. Then in the silence of my car, this thought emerged. Now I know I can trust you. *When I say go, you will go. When I say follow me, I know you will follow me. Even if you do not know where you are going. Even if you do not know why. Even if you are alone. And even if you are afraid, you will follow me.*

Miles are adding up in the distance and two new thoughts are uncovered. They lie naked in my mind. My creased lines on my face softened as my lips formed the slightest smile. Yes, Lord. Yes, Lord. Let's.

THIRTY-NINE

August 2018
Dear Jesus,

I am caught in a net. I am seeing only things that surround me. What I see surrounding me is sin and brokenness. Hurt, strife, and struggle. Once I stepped all in following hard after You, I learned I have an enemy. You see the enemy did not care about me when I was living my own life for myself. I was not a threat to him, but today, that changed. The moment I began sharing the good news with anyone who would listen was the day he showed up on my doorstep. I am not going to lie, it is terrifying when all you can see is the disaster encircling you; however, You have showed me something beyond what I can see. You are giving me glimpses beyond my circumstances.

It all started when my fear was bigger than my faith and You gifted me with a cardinal. Then another. Then another. To me the cardinal symbolizes, "Those who are with us are more than those who are with them." My real fear is being hurt, traumatized, taunted, and vandalized by someone I once knew. My real fear is being physically, emotionally, mentally, and spiritually hurt. But God. The first eight cardinals appeared in my backyard. Then a cardinal appeared in a kiosk at the mall with the words written on it, "When angels are near, cardinals appear." Then a cardinal appeared in my mailbox, with the words written on it, "Be still and know that I am God." All these cardinals appeared on the same day. The next morning, there were cardinals sitting in the bush outside my garage side entrance door. There were cardinals surrounding my dog kennel. Every morning when I drive out of my driveway, cardinals fly overhead. One day I was waiting to pick up my kids from school and a cardinal almost flew into my open window! I was making bouquets for my brother-in-law's wedding and a cardinal sat perched on a wire outside the porch window. This seems ridiculous, Jesus, but it is happening all the same. It is occurring daily and the more people I share this with, the more cardinals there are.

Lord, You are God and You can do anything. There is no one like You. Some believe in horses and some trust in chariots, but I believe and trust in You. What I know is I sought You, and You answered me; You delivered me from all my fears. Those who look to You are radiant; their faces never covered with shame. (Ps. 34:4) Fear. But God. I am so thankful I asked You to reveal the outer circle, the space beyond what I can see. Thank You that You are delighted to do so. You did it for the servant in 2 Kings 6 and You did it for me.

> Then he sent horses and chariots and a strong force there. They went by night and surrounded the city. When the servant of the man of God got up and went out early the next morning, an army with horses and chariots had surrounded the city. "Oh no, my lord! What shall we do?" the servant asked. "Don't be afraid," the prophet answered. "Those who are with us are more than those who are with them." And Elisha prayed, "Open his eyes, LORD, so that he may see." Then the LORD opened the servant's eyes, and he looked and saw the hills full of horses and chariots of fire all around Elisha.
>
> 2 Kings 6:14–17

"Some trust in chariots and some in horses, but we trust in the name of the LORD our God" (Psalm 20:7).

FORTY

September 20, 2018
Dear Jesus,

I am learning to replace fear with trust. Learning how to do this is hard and has been ongoing. I want to trust when I cannot see. As my trust strengthens in one area, I see You move on to new areas where I can deepen my relationship with You and trust You more. My story reveals the power of You, Christ, and how You long to redeem and restore us.

A couple months ago, I made an appointment with my doctor's office. Before I made the appointment, I researched a new physician. I have not had the best results with doctors or diagnoses, and I felt I needed to start fresh. I needed to find someone I could trust, a woman preferably. I found a name and dialed and made the appointment, which was long overdue. I wanted to make the appointment a few weeks down the road, so I could shed those few extra pounds before I stepped on the dreaded doctor's office scale which by the way adds at least five pounds if not ten. Unfortunately, the appointment was made for later in the week—so much for dropping a few.

As the day neared, I began to feel nervous. I knew the appointment was long overdue. Annual physicals are never fun, but beyond that I was going to have to get transparent and reveal my messed-up life and my failing physical and emotional health. There were so many topics. How was I ever going to hit them all? Thankfully, my mom headed to the park with my children, as I slowly drove across the street to the clinic. I began to sweat as I took my seat in the waiting area. As the nurse appeared in the doorway, I stood and walked forward. As I entered the open doorway, I rounded the corner to the dreaded black scale. I stepped on backwards, a little trick I learned during my pregnancies, but unfortunately, the nurse did not take to my clue and spoke the dreaded numbers out loud. My clothes began to absorb my sweat. As I sat in the stale off white room, my eyes made shapes with the tiles on the floor as I began answering questions. Then I heard something I would like to take back.

She said, "So, it has been six years since your last pap, and it was abnormal?" My mind raced. Questions flew about silently. What? What was happening? My clothes now went from damp to drenched. That cannot be right! I finally spoke out loud. "I know it has been a while, but six years?" I questioned.

"Yes," she stated bluntly.

"Okay," I mouthed.

She finished typing in my answers and left the room. I wanted to cry. Run. I wanted to be anywhere but there. I undressed and put on the silly robe. I still do not know if it ties in the front or back. Whatever. I sat naked in a weird sheet waiting for my physician. My doctor entered and smiled. She said sweetly, "Oh, shoot. You did not need to undress. I always like to meet my patients first."

Perfect, I thought.

She began asking me questions and I had a bad moment. The worst moment. I fell apart right there with a woman I did not know. I laid my soul bare in her presence. She was so kind and compassionate. It did not matter. I was still a wreck. When it came time for my pap, I could barely lie still. Then I heard more words I would like to take back. She voiced, "This is what a normal uterus looks like. And this is what yours looks like." Tears rolled down my cheeks. She asked me if I was always like this. "Yes," I said surprising myself. "I think I am."

Two months have passed since this office visit. My uterus turned out to be simply fine, thank You, Jesus. Two months ago, I began a new medication. A medication I am not ashamed of. A round white pill I am so grateful for. I have hope that with this new medication,

I may be able to heal completely. Two years I have grieved. I am so grateful I went straight through the pain and I am glad I experienced every emotion and every let down. You have been so faithful and near. I have never been alone because You walked me through this wilderness one day at a time and You are still walking with me. You have taught me so many truths in Your word that I have applied to my heart, but I have learned something else: you can know the truth, apply the truth to your heart and still not be living free in Christ. I was held captive in a shell. The guard rails were up. I was held captive in a prison. My prison. My body had become my prison. I had the knowledge of Your word, my heart was soft and I knew the truth; however, my body was not working in unison with my mind and heart thus I was missing out on Your perfect joy, peace, and stability.

I believe I have found some help. Thank You for providing me with the medication I need to help undo the damage to my mind and body. Each day I take this round, white pill, I am grateful. Every day I feel my clenched body begin to relax and I feel myself breathing again. I have been holding my breath for two years. Two years. I want to breathe again, and I want to walk freely in the life You have prepared for me. Help me take my guard rails down. I do not want to do more or be more. I want to sit with You and allow You to free my soul.

FORTY-ONE

September 2018
Dear Jesus,

Last summer, I had the event of a lifetime. I was going home to a family wedding. It was on my father's side of the family. I had not seen this family since the broken relationship with my father. For weeks leading up to the trip, I was ill. My stomach was in knots, my mind felt chaotic, and I was a complete jittery mess. I knew I had to go. I knew You were restoring pieces of me, Lord, and this was part of Your plan. It was another stretching step for me. God, I had so many questions. Who would I see? What would they think of me? Would I have to defend myself? Would they believe me? Would they still love me?

The day of departure arrived and I was a mess. Sitting in the car I could barely breathe. My palms were sweating, and I believe I had a death grip on Brandon's hand the whole way. Somewhere along the way, even though there was pain, something new began to emerge. There was a desire to make new memories with my family. We took old traditions and made them new. Pieces of my past began to have a new place in my future, and it all started with a Maid-Rite and the people I adore.

I am not going to lie. The whole weekend was unnerving. There were beautiful pieces of redemption, but pain was right there with it all. The day of the wedding came, and it was time to see family without my dad. It was wrong. So wrong. It made me grieve sin and this broken world we live in. It made me desire a place where there is only love and beautiful light. My family welcomed me with open arms. I did not have to defend myself because You, Jesus, are my defender. Truth and pain were present on my face, but Your love, Lord, covered it all. I did not tell my side of the story or speak poorly of anyone or any event that happened. The only thing I did at this wedding was participate in love and truth.

When my uncle got up to give his father/daughter speech, the lump in my throat swelled to bursting. The pain was so palpable. I walked over to the mother of the bride and sat on the floor near her, holding her hand with soft tears rolling down my cheeks. Joy and pain intermingled. At one point, I watched one of my son's dance with a girl on the dance floor which made my cheeks hurt so much from smiling. Brandon and I were the only ones who could understand this beautiful, strange feeling. An intimate moment between the two of us. New memories were being made. New bonds. New life made in truth and only truth. It felt good to uncover the dust.

As we were driving home from the wedding a thought settled on my heart. You do not need to say anything to be a light. People can see love and truth written in your spirit.

> You are the light of the world. A town built on a hill cannot be hidden. Neither do people light a lamp and put it under a bowl. Instead they put it on its stand, and it gives light to everyone in the house. In the same way, let your light shine before others, that they may see your good deeds and glorify your Father in heaven.
> Matthew 5:14–16

FORTY-TWO

September 2018
Dear Jesus,

Sifting. This is what I have been doing the last couple of years. Sifting through the years. What is the truth? What are the lies? I am sifting through the puzzle pieces of my life putting them back together one at a time. There are a lot of memories. Lots of thoughts. Lots of broken, jagged pieces.

There has been one memory that has haunted me. I have thought about it many times throughout my life. It is one of those memories that just does not leave. It just hangs out there in that floating space in my mind, hovering. Shortly after my parents got divorced, my dad began seeing a new woman. Surprisingly, I adored her. She had the smile that lit up a room and eyes that sparkled. She called me "Baby-girl" in a loving way with a slightly Southern accent that I loved. I remember spending a lot of time with her. I can still hear the drums from a Wilson Phillips cassette tape playing over and over as I rode around in her car that one summer. I liked the thought of this woman in my life and then instantly it was snatched away. This pattern would play an integral part of my life. Getting close, loving something or someone, and then the object or person would disappear, and a story would follow. In this instance, I was told my lovely mother figure was a bank robber. How could someone with a smile like that and eyes that sparkled be a bank robber? This jagged, broken puzzle piece did not fit.

I had the opportunity to connect with this woman and I could have typed something to her, but I needed to speak to this woman, and I needed to know it was her for sure. I needed to hear her voice. I needed to know everything. I was terrified, but I punched in those numbers trembling. When she answered, I eked out my name. What followed blew me back thirty years. "Baby-girl." In one word, I knew. *Everything.* She loved me. *Always. Still.* How? Why? Why was she snatched from me? Why did my father tell me she robbed the bank? Eventually, throughout the conversation, the edge of the puzzle piece softened and was neatly put back together.

Lord, You are amazing. You are the God of restoration. You are redeeming my story for your glory. Your story is about God conquering evil and redeeming Your people. It is not about me at all. It is Your redemption story for Your glory. You did restore and redeem me through this situation, but it was not about me. It was about You and Your plan and Your purpose. I was just written in the pages and was willing to be used. As You restore my life I have had to die to self and in doing so, I am being made new. The old is gone and the new has come. When I follow You and Your plan for my life, I will know the truth and the truth will set me free. This has been so hard for me, but healing at the same time. As I reveal my hurts and true heart's desire in accordance with Your will, I know restoration will follow.

"And the God of all grace, who called you to his eternal glory in Christ, after you have suffered a little while, will himself restore you and make you strong, firm, and steadfast" (1 Pet. 5:10).

FORTY-THREE

October 2018
Dear Jesus,

I had just returned from the Northwestern Christian Writing Conference last summer. Coming home, I had so many questions I had to ask You. I came home like a noodle. Limp and wet. The writing conference stretched me to the max. Not just the conference itself, but the experience of doing it alone. Steven Furtick said it well, "Coming into your calling means coming out of your comfort zone." I was completely over the line. Comfort was not in my vocabulary. Your calling is clear, but to be transparent, share, and speak out is not comfortable for me at all. What I am doing is obeying Your Spirit. Period. Coming into my calling has given me beautiful views of Your perspective, but it has also shown me not everyone will understand my calling. Everyone has been given God given gifts and when people radically follow You to obey, it sometimes looks asinine. I have thought about others, been on the judging team not the grace team, but I like Your perspective. Go for it! I am with you! Why are Christians so eager to judge others? Why are we so eager to pull those soaring for You to the floor? Why are we threatened when others are doing great things for Your great name?

Once home and recovered from my trip, something awesome happened. I put on a new attribute: bravery. I dawned the bravery hat everywhere I went. I was a new woman, free to be me, the Jesus-loving girl who was now every bit stretched to real. I was sitting on the cold, hard bleachers watching a baseball game when another mother came over and was showing off a new piercing. I was stunned. You just went in on a whim and did it? I have wanted cartilage piercings since I was a fourteen-year-old girl. I have wanted a tattoo since I was eighteen and a specially designed tattoo since I had my fourth child. I sat with the paper print out of the tattoo I designed waiting to be birthed. In the past, I had stated it would never happen because I was too afraid of what people would think of me. What would the church members think? What would my children think? What would my husband think? But God. You stretched me to be real.

The following week, I marched straight into a tattoo and piercing parlor and had three cartilage piercings done. Painful, yes. Liberating, even more yes. I was set free. Two weeks later, I walked into another tattoo shop and went into my scheduled tattoo appointment. I walked out thirty minutes later marked. Freedom blew my hair back and smacked a smile across my face that would not be removed for days. Why did I wait so long? Fear. Fear and bondage. People pleasing had me held hostage. You have set me free.

I walked into my chiropractor's office on a Friday morning. When he saw my piercings and tattoo, he asked if I was having a mid-life crisis, having just turned forty. I said, "No. I am finally okay with just being me. I don't care what other's think of me anymore." I finished this appointment and then went to a coffee shop to meet a dear friend. It was hot. It was summer. I dawned a tank top that sported my new ink. When I walked back from refilling my coffee my friend questioned my tattoo. "Have you always had that? Is it new?"

"Brand new," I stated with the grin that would not leave my face. We giggled. We then joked about returning to Bible study in the fall with me all pierced and tatted up. What would the women think? She came up with a new nickname for me. Her Jesus-loving, bad*** friend. I walked out of that coffee shop with the most breezy feeling. I was floating on the freedom You have provided. There was no more fear. I was not afraid of what people thought of me any longer.

Study commenced and looked like it was going to be another beautiful time of God's word, fellowship, and transparency. It did not last long. Something was wrong. You could cut the tension with a knife. Our study had turned from vulnerable to surface in seconds. There was no more real sharing. It had been replaced by surface stones. The enemy had been prowling and found his foothold. Religion, idolatry, comparison, and unforgiven past hurts. Then something unthinkable happened. I was questioned and accused right there in the middle of a church with a table full of Christians. This blind spot lingered, and I was invited to lunch. My leading became a topic and I was blindsided. I was told that as a leader, I needed to work on the amount I shared. I was told that I needed to think of myself above the group, not better, but above. I was not to share too much weakness. If I needed to share, I should spill it privately to the leadership. And then the unthinkable happened. I was questioned on my ability to lead due to my emotional stability. A place where I was called to be transparent quickly became unsafe and my pearl had been trampled.

Fear of people crept back in. *I cannot be real. I cannot be transparent. I cannot lead. I am not good enough.* Then I heard the good news:

> The God of our ancestors has chosen you to know his will and to see the Righteous One and to hear words from his mouth. You will be his witness to all people of what you have seen and heard.
> Acts 22:14–15

And then I heard, "Rather, he made himself nothing by taking the very nature of a servant, being made in human likeness" (Phil. 2:7). Thank You for reminding me that I am to share what You are doing. I am to obey my calling. I am in a very vulnerable position. The Spirit is asking me to share the words and trials He has given me. Believe me, I would rather sit and not share and not speak of my weaknesses, trials, and temptations, but when You call, I obey.

I will never sit around a table with a group of women and think of myself as better. I will be like You, making myself nothing by taking the very nature of a servant. You are the one I am following and no one else.

Your real, Jesus-loving girl was scrolling Etsy the other day looking for a Christmas gift. What popped on the screen flushed my cheeks rosy. A Morris-code friendship bracelet that spelled out bad***. I tried to back out and go to a different screen, but then I returned quickly. I put two in the cart and mailed one off to my girlfriend. This is where I want to be, Jesus. Free in Christ. Not sinning, reckless, and out of control, but true, real, and vulnerable. This is where the church needs to be. Rooted in Christ and boldly declaring the gospel in love.

> Therefore, there is now no condemnation for those who are in Christ Jesus, because through Christ Jesus the law of the Spirit who gives life has set you free from the law of sin and death. For what the law was powerless to do because it was weakened by the flesh, God did by sending his own Son in the likeness of sinful flesh to be a sin offering. And so, he condemned sin in the flesh, in order that the righteous requirement of the law might be fully met in us, who do not live according to the flesh but according to the Spirit.
>
> Romans 8:1–4

FORTY-FOUR

November 2018
Dear Jesus,

It came on a Sunday morning. The answer I had been waiting for. My last test result had entered my inbox. When I read the results, I was not surprised. I had read this word my entire life. *Normal.* Oh, how I had hoped. Hoped for an answer. Hoped for guidance. Hoped for closure. Is this my thorn? Have I given up on You? Is everything I have written so far worthless? Are You still not worthy to be praised?

Jesus, You are still Lord of my life. I hear You so clearly. I will fight for you. You need only to be still. In quiet and trust will be my strength. (Isa. 30:15)

The other day, I sat down and wrote a speech. I have no idea why I did this or who these words would help. I had a lot on my heart, and I needed to pour it out onto the pages. Everything I had learned from You I had to spill out to Your people in hopes of breaking the walls of religion down. I wanted to share truth. So, something I hated doing in high school and college I willingly sat down in enjoyment to do. You placed it on my heart to share in front of a large group of women. I went to the leadership of the Bible study I attended and asked if I could share my testimony. I was met with a resounding, "Yes." The speech was transparent and personal and written for Your glory. Much of the story included information about my health and some of my emotional distress after extensive emotional abuse. After a lunch date weeks later, I was questioned on my emotional stability and my ability to lead. This stung, but I heard, "I will fight for you. You need only to be still" (Ps. 46:10).

A few weeks later, I sat in my doctor's office to go over my new medication. I was struggling with feelings of anxiety and more anxiety than I had before I started the medication. Before the appointment, my doctor prescribed another medication to take in conjunction with the first medication. I had taken this new medication a few times before the visit. At the appointment, I was vocal about my disgust of the clenching feeling I was having. I thought I was having a side effect of the medication, but instead a third medication was prescribed.

My doctor asked me if I needed to see a therapist. I told her I had been seeing a family member who is a Christian counselor. I noticed a slight smirk. You know me, Lord. I called the smirk out. "Is this not good enough?" She moved her hand in a circular motion hovering over the paper and said, "If this doesn't work, then you are going to a psychiatrist and a therapist." We continued talking about her medication plan for me and I asked her if she knew of a Christian therapist she could recommend to me. I have nothing against being well and being willing to try new recommendations. She told me it was not her specialty. The smirk returned, and I heard, "Do the two have to go together?" I clearly told her that I could not separate my faith and healing process. She said, "Isn't that what your faith is supposed to do for you? Give you peace?" I walked out. I prayed. I waited to follow Your lead, was eventually able to eliminate all medication and the anxiety stopped and I heard, "I will fight for you. You need only to be still."

Why would anyone in the church want to share their testimony if it is spewed back in their face? Why would anyone share their faith when it is mocked? Christians *do* still hurt and grieve. Can You believe that? I do have a thorn, Jesus. It keeps me grounded in Your Word. It keeps me close to truth. I have struggled a lifetime without a diagnosis and topped it off with emotional abuse at the hand of a loved one. I am weak. I have never denied this truth, but when I am weak, then I am strong. Jesus, You are the one fighting for me and it is not about me at all. It is all for Your redemption story.

FORTY-FIVE

November 2018
Dear Jesus,

Why would I go somewhere where I knew the invitee's motives were not pure? When questions in my mind flood in like, *why would they be inviting me over? They have never done this before. Did I do something wrong? Should I go?* Then I walk myself through what to do and not to do in any given situation. What I should talk about and what are the forbidden topics trying to protect myself before I ever enter their home? As I entered a home under these circumstances, I noticed a few subtle topics that conflicted with my biblical view of the Word. I sat silently and tried to give Spirit-led answers. Somehow, someway the conversation entered the forbidden territory. I began using words carefully. The conversation took an unexpected turn and I became bothered. Offended and accused. I left as soon as I was able. I began driving and rehearsing and then realized I have just entered an uncomfortable situation. A situation that should have been avoided. A situation where following You is the only option and in doing so, I separate myself out yet again, standing on truth.

I have done this so many times. The stinker is when I do this, I miss the Spirit's leading. The Spirit goes before me. He gives me the first question mark. Yet I go anyway. I then have one or two or three cues from the Spirit that I ignore. Then out comes this jumbled, way out of proportion, unbiblical, non-gospel centered quarrel that cannot be ignored because walking with You is non-negotiable. How do I not only hear the Spirit's leading, but learn to quickly obey it, protecting my pearl? I want to believe people. I want to trust leaders and fellow church members' leading; however, I am convicted of this thought. The Holy Spirit is enough. He is the voice of truth. He is the one guiding me and going before me to protect me and His holy message. The last time this happened to me, I had to take a step back and look at the similarity in these types of situations and ask for Your help. You are always available to help me, and You want to protect me. When I do not listen to You, I make myself available to attacks, accusations, grief, loss, and separation. Help me to be quick to obey the Spirit's leading and help me be still and know You are fighting for me. Jesus, help me be like You and when I am accused help me give no answer. Today, I sit quietly in truth waiting and listening for Your guiding. I wish I would have listened to Your promptings. If I had, I would not be in this situation.

A beautiful Christian song came into my email after I excused myself from the unhealthy visit. I have heard this song a million times and I enjoy it; however, in this situation I was accused by the enemy to my core. The words in this situation were hurtful. I cried calling out to You in my distress. I have been serving You, Lord, and leading Your people. Why would I be accused surrounded by believers? Why? Why? Why? Please help me! The separation and accusations I have endured are endless and painful. As I was crying out to You, I subtly heard, "You will see the goodness of the Lord in the land of the living." I heard it four times. My tears broke, and I looked up. Thank You. You went before me, prepared me, and answered me quickly. I pulled over and typed in the words I heard to find the scripture reference.

"I remain confident of this: I will see the goodness of the LORD IN the land of the living. Wait for the LORD; be strong and take heart and wait for the LORD" (Ps. 27:13–14).

Sometimes I need to slow down, listen, ask, and listen some more. I am a sheep. Thank You for Your faithful, constant, guidance.

"The Lord himself goes before you and will be with you; he will never leave you nor forsake you. Do not be afraid; do not be discouraged" (Deut. 31:8).

FORTY-SIX

November 28, 2018
Dear Jesus,

I am going to get straight to the point. I have an accuser who is the father of lies active in my daily life looking to distract and disarm me. He comes at me in all forms looking for an inch of space to be invited in. He comes through my loved ones, church members, fellow leaders, and friends. This has been a hard pill for me to swallow. How can he accuse me through fellow Christians? As I have become aware of the accuser, I have seen his lies directed at me. The beautiful thing is when I became aware of the accuser, I became the one disarming him. I will praise You, Jesus!

You have given me many examples in my own life as to how he accuses me and others.

I have a dear friend being accused daily in her own home by the person who is supposed to love and cherish her. Daily she hears lies about who she is. She hears she is worthless. She hears that everyone would be better off without her. She hears that she is awful. She hears that she is not good enough. She hears there is no purpose for her.

I have a dear friend being accused daily in her own home by the children she cares for. She hears you are lazy. She hears you love them more than you love me. She hears you do not care about me. She hears nothing she does is ever good enough.

I have a dear friend being accused daily in her own home that her choices are hurting the family. She hears she is just like her father. She hears she is unworthy to care for her children. She hears she is never going to be good enough.

I have a dear friend who is being accused daily of her life choices.

She hears because of one act of humanness she is not forgiven. She hears she will never be clean. She hears she is not worthy to mingle with godly Christ followers. She hears she is weak.

I have a dear friend who is being accused daily that she is not good enough. She hears she is unequipped. She hears she is unqualified. She hears she is inadequate to lead. She hears everyone is better than her.

I have a dear friend who is being accused daily that she is not a good friend. She hears she said too much. She hears she is ungodly. She hears she is unworthy of friendship. She hears she is not following Christ appropriately. She hears she is a mistake.

These are the lies I hear, and other women hear and are believing. This makes me so mad. I want to tell everyone that these are lies. I am no longer going to believe these lies and I am going to get into the word and fill my life and mind with truth. Truth I am going to believe and treasure. I am going to say every time I hear a lie: I am beautiful, special, loved, designed, created for purpose, important, forgiven, protected, and chosen. I am a daughter of the King. I am a victor not a victim. Who the son sets free is free indeed. Satan is under my feet.

"Let the king be enthralled by your beauty; honor him, for he is your lord" (Ps. 45:11).

"For you created my inmost being, you knit me together in my mother's womb" (Ps. 139:13).

"I have loved you with an everlasting love; I have drawn you with unfailing kindness" (Jer. 31:3).

> So that Christ may dwell in your hearts through faith. And I pray that you, being rooted and established in love, may have power, together with all the Lord's holy people, to grasp how wide and long and high and deep is the love of Christ, and to know this love that surpasses knowledge—that you may be filled to the measure of all the fullness of God.

Ephesians 3:17–19

"But you are a chosen people, a royal priesthood, a holy nation, God's special possession, that you may declare the praises of him who called you out of darkness into his wonderful light" (1 Pet. 2:9).

"As far as the east is from the west, so far has he removed our transgressions from us" (Ps. 103:12).

"He will not let your foot slip— he who watches over you will not slumber" (Ps. 121:3).

"You did not choose me, but I chose you and appointed you so that you might go and bear fruit—fruit that will last—and so that whatever you ask in my name the Father will give you" (John 15:16).

"Be alert and of sober mind. Your enemy the devil prowls around like a roaring lion looking for someone to devour" (1 Pet. 5:8).

Then I heard a loud voice in heaven say: "Now have come the salvation and the power and the kingdom of our God, and the authority of his Messiah. For the accuser of our brothers and sisters, who accuses them before our God day and night, has been hurled down."

Revelation 12:10

"The God of peace will soon crush Satan under my feet" (Rom. 16:20).

FORTY-SEVEN

December 2018
Dear Jesus,

I heard You loud and clear. You need to follow me and only me. All at once, Jesus, I lost my father, my church family, and one of my best friends. My husband could not help me either and just when I needed them the most, You removed them from me. Jesus, You have separated me out and I feel alone. What I was left with was enough though. You, Jesus, are enough for me. Had You not separated me out, I would not have begun writing with Your word and found my purpose in You. I would not have found satisfaction, contentment, and my abundant life.

You formed me and knew me before I was born. You set me apart. This setting apart and removal and shaping and lonely feeling hurts so deeply, but I know it is for Your divine purpose. I believe You want me and all of me and anything that gets in the way You will remove. You do it for all Your children because You are a jealous God for us. You love us too much to leave us short of our designed purpose.

I have had so many feelings, thoughts, and so many unanswered questions, but ultimately the only thing I was left with was trust. I trust You so much, Jesus, that I believe You when You speak to me. I am willing to give up my life, my comfort to stand with You and only You. I hear You so clearly reminding me to act justly, love mercy, and humbly walk with You. I have done these things faithfully still hurting and watching others hurt. Being separate sometimes feels unloving, but I hear You continue to ask me to love being separate. I believe I have loved and sought after people and things above You

Father. Forgive me.

Events happen. Crisis happens. Many times, news of hard times crush my soul and I cry and pray for people You have removed. I want to run and love people closely, but I hear You still, "You can love and be separate." I have learned following You is a choice. I choose to follow even when I do not know where I am going. One day I hope I understand completely, but until then I choose to trust You know what You are doing.

"Naked I came from my mother's womb, and naked I will depart. The LORD gave and the LORD has taken away; may the name of the LORD be praised" (Job 1:21)

FORTY-EIGHT

December 12, 2018
Dear Jesus,

It appeared. Soft and subtle. *You must prepare the field.* I let the dust settle for a few days. I continue to hear those words. *You must prepare the field.* So, I am writing a story without the ending. Scary. I heard You clearly. Your story matters. I am restoring you completely. Your life, health, marriage, and family will be restored, and You will give me the glory. You consistently ask me to believe when I cannot see. So, I am willingly writing a book about my restoration even though I do not know how it will end. It reminds me of a painful time, sixteen years ago, of trusting without seeing.

Brandon and I were newlyweds and we were building our first house. He designed this house for us, and I was ecstatic about the two pink lines I just saw. I remember scrutinizing over the white stick. Is there another pink line? Why is it so faint? I just sat and stared at it. I looked in the kitchen light, the bathroom light, next to the window with the sunlight. Then I bought more and scrutinized over all of them. I had two girlfriends examine them. It was true. I was pregnant. I was happy. Beyond happy.

It did not last long. Early on in my pregnancy, I started spotting. Doctors told me it would be okay. People told me it would be okay, but deep down I knew it was not going to be okay. I was losing the baby. I have never felt such emotional pain in my life. Brandon found me on the couch when he returned from work crumpled in a ball. I cried out to You, Lord. Why? Why? Why? Did I do something wrong? Did I drink too much caffeine? Exercise too much? It was true. My heart was broken.

Shortly after my first miscarriage, I became pregnant again. Worry consumed me. More medical testing was done, and doctors assured me the baby was fine. When I went in for the ultrasound to check on the baby there was a heartbeat and the baby was healthy. The time came for our baby to arrive. He came three weeks early and it was the second-best day of my life after marrying Brandon. Kristian James Orloff was perfect. He was better than I could have ever imagined. I always imagined him having light skin like me and barely any blonde hair. Not Kristian! He had beautiful olive skin like his dad and a full head of dark hair. He was beautiful. I never wanted to stop looking at him. I was in love.

We wanted more children and I became pregnant around the time Kristian was one year old. Again, I was beyond excited. These were the best days of my life so far, but early on in my pregnancy I began spotting again. This time I did not even ask. I knew. I was losing this baby too. I cried out to You, Lord. Why? Why? Why? Again, that terrible feeling of loss overwhelmed me. That feeling of guilt. That feeling of being responsible for the loss. The pressure of feeling like I should have done something differently and I would have been able to keep the two babies I lost.

Shortly after, I became pregnant with Jakob Brandon Orloff. He looked just like me; blonde and fair. He was breathtaking. I loved being a new mom and I loved the family that You gifted me with. Eventually I had two more children, Lukas Gray and Ella Rose. Precious and perfect. Nothing could have prepared me for the love I felt for my children. The only thing that would have been better is if the two babies I lost could have lived here on earth with us. Through the years I studied Your word, prayed, and sought Your wisdom on miscarriage. I believe my family will be united with the two Orloff babes in heaven one day. I shared this truth with my children and then with another mom as she began a journey of miscarriage of her own.

What happened through this testimony caught me off guard.

Forty-Eight

One of my children came to the saving grace of Jesus Christ through this trial. A nine-year-old boy who did not know why he needed Jesus before. A nine-year-old boy who thought he was good enough. A nine-year-old boy who learned the truth. "For all have sinned and fall short of the glory of God" (Rom. 3:23). A nine-year-old boy who wrote out a beautiful testimony etched with some of my deepest scars for His glory. My son stood up on the stage and boldly read his handwritten testimony, then was buried with Christ and rose to new life. I believe this: "And we know that in all things God works for the good of those who love him, who have been called according to his purpose rings true for me" (Rom. 8:28).

I know without a doubt You hear me. Not a tear goes by unnoticed. You died on the cross and took the pain for me. As I call out to You, You not only hear me, but You take my personal requests and work them for my good and for Your purpose. You heard me that day crumpled on my couch and then You gave me the courage and truth to share my testimony with people I care about. You transferred some of my deepest pain to a beautiful love story. A story of God redeeming His people. My son is a testimony to that. I will wait expectantly to be reunited with my children in heaven as one. Trusting without seeing is what faith is all about. I will write this book and wait expectantly. Trusting without seeing the outcome.

FORTY-NINE

December 12, 2018
Dear Jesus,

I never want to be shallow again. I never want to sit on the surface again. I never want to hold my testimony again. I never want to be complacent. What I want is to go deep because deep is where You are. I do not want to just hear a message. I want to move. Move following You wherever You are calling me. I want to shout from the rooftops the praise due Your name. I want to tell all people what a wonderful, beautiful Savior You are. I am no longer scared. I no longer am afraid of people. I am moved solely by Your Spirit. Grounded in the word, yes! Held accountable by other believers, yes, but on the move! You have been whispering to me while I sleep. I hear You whisper it is not about what you do or do not do. I want you. Period. Sit with me. Just sit here with me. Let me fill you with my awesome power and love. Sit where you not only are able to hear but listen. Drown out the noise and sit in my presence. I know I am not alone. I see You move daily because I am seeking You with my whole heart. I am running hard after You the race marked out for me.

A few years ago, we were living with my brother-in-law, and his wife, while we were building our new house. There were eight people, a few cats, two dogs and a litter of ten puppies living under one roof with one bathroom! What this means is that it was pure chaos. We packed our house into their house and just moved right in. God bless their hearts! I set up a temporary computer station in one of the downstairs rooms. One morning, I had driven my two oldest boys to school and had returned to do a couple of hours of work for our plumbing business. Lukas and Ella were playing around me while I worked in my makeshift office. Lukas reached for a bag of crayons and the next thing I knew I was laying over Ella crumpled on the floor with a concrete-filled door on top of us. How did I get here? What happened? I have no idea. I shoved off the door, collected my two precious gems and rushed to the living room. Blood was rushing out of Ella's head and I screamed out the door for my brother-in-law. He rushed us all to the hospital. Only a small corner of the door sliced her head. Ella had a few staples put in and she was fine. The heavy door did not touch her. It hit me square in the back of my head. I do not even want to know what would have happened if I had not been there.

What is the explanation? There is only one. You. We were not alone that morning. Somehow, I made it across the room and placed my body over her before I ever knew anything was happening. See what I mean? How can I keep quiet? I want to shout it from the rooftops. When you pass through the waters, He will be with you! "When you pass through the rivers, they will not sweep over you. When you walk through the fire, you will not be burned; the flames will not set you ablaze." (Is. 43:2). You are watching over us. Protecting us every minute of every day. I cannot explain it, but I am thankful I opened my heart to see it and receive it. You are worthy of our praise.

Recently I was asked to keep my sharing to a minimum. Even typing these words make me feel bad, hurt, unworthy. I believe You have called me to speak. I believe You have gifted me with the ability to appropriate Your word to daily living. These words caused a battle in my thoughts. Do I talk too much? Am I sharing too much? Is it beneficial? Is it drawing others to Jesus? But then. Truth pierced the lie. Just like Ella, Lukas, and I were not alone in that office, I did not fight this battle in my mind alone. You have been so faithful to fill me with life breathing words. Words I want others to know. You have called me to share. To be transparent. To go deep. Here is what Your word says:

"It has seemed good to me to show the signs and wonders that the Most-High God has done for me" (Dan. 4:2 ESV).

"And they have conquered him by the blood of the Lamb and by the word of their testimony, for they loved not their lives even unto death" (Rev. 12:11 ESV).

"Oh, give thanks to the Lord; call upon his name; make known his deeds among the peoples!" (1 Chr. 16:8 ESV).

"Let the redeemed of the Lord say so, whom he has redeemed from trouble" (Ps. 107:2 ESV).

"But you will receive power when the Holy Spirit has come upon you, and you will be my witness in Jerusalem and in all Judea and Samaria, and to the end of the earth" (Acts 1:8 ESV).

"And he did not permit him but said to him, 'Go home to your friends and tell them how much the Lord has done for you, and how he has had mercy on you'" (Mark 5:19 ESV).

"I will also speak of your testimonies before kings and shall not be put to shame" (Ps. 119:46 ESV).

"I will tell of your name to my brothers; in the midst of the congregation I will sing your praise" (Heb. 2:12 ESV).

You, Jesus, are doing great things. I will shout it out. I will tell the people what You have done for me. I will praise Your holy name. For You are good, all-powerful, a mighty counselor, and sovereign. I am never alone. I will seek You with my whole heart and jump at the chance to share the good news.

FIFTY

January 2019
Dear Jesus,

This day had been coming for a long time. I believe the time has come for me to join social media. I have always been too shy and too private, and I never wanted to be transparent or vulnerable and especially in public. Somewhere along the broken road I fell in love with You, Jesus, and You started asking me to share. I never heard You ask me aloud, but in the depth of my soul I knew what You wanted from me. You wanted me to share my unstable walk and tell it 100 percent real.

The first time I ever shared was in my small church from the last red-lined pew. The pastor read a verse and asked us if or how this passage affected us. I slowly stood waiting for the microphone with five pair of eyes looking at me begging me to sit down. Believe me, I wanted to sit down, but I knew You gave this word for me to share. I fumbled with the microphone, stammered out some unintelligible words, and even shed a tear or two. I passed the microphone on and sat down. I never thought I would recover. My heart was racing, I was sweating and breathing heavily. Those ten eyes were staring straight ahead, but I believed I knew what they were thinking. Why? Why did you do that? I wondered too. In the car a few weeks later, one of my sons asked me why I did it and followed his question by another question wondering if I was scared. For me, this is where my faith became reality, and visible and then passed down to the next generation. I responded to my son's sincere questions. "I felt like God wanted me to share how He was working in my life so that He could encourage others. And yes,

I was terrified."

No one in the car responded. No one in church ever said anything to me about my testimony that day. Jesus, this left me feeling exposed and naked. I felt judged and I doubted why I did it. A couple months later, I ran into a woman from church at the grocery store. There she shared how much my words encouraged her. One other person commented how my words impacted her and encouraged her to look up His words that I shared in the poem "I Will" inspired by the book of Isaiah. I would love to impact many people for Your namesake, but I am learning slowly that if sharing You only affects three people, then it is only for three. Being uncomfortable for the sake of the gospel is starting to feel worth it.

I continued standing and taking a microphone now and then. Each time I felt reckless inside, but knew it was all for Your glory. I have had to learn that what You think of me is all that matters. You really scrawled this on my soul the day my father began telling lies about me and my family. I had to learn that our identity does not come from our parents, our siblings, friends, or mentors. Our identity comes from Christ and Christ alone. As You continue to refine me, You ask me to continue to be transparent in front of others. I do this with my writing, in Bible study and in my daily life, but now? I sense You asking me to display it on social media. Before I shared with other Christ-followers, friends, and family members—people I chose to share with. Now I am sharing to a watching world who You put in my path.

It all started when someone I knew shared their adoption story on a private Facebook page. After a while I got tired of asking for updates and I believe You have been nudging me to join social media this past year, but this was the final shove I needed. I jumped. All in. I thought everything was great until I heard You ask me to share a vulnerable post. I am not going to lie. I did not sleep a wink. I felt anxious right to the center of my core. I felt naked and raw and would love to do any and everything to cover up. I still do. However, I keep hearing You. *People need to know. People need to know me. Not religion. Not rules. They need to know I love them. I chose them. I am here for them. I died for them even while they were still sinners* (Rom. 5:8). So, I press on.

I had my ugly prayer time with You the other night. Why. Why me? So many people are more equipped than me. So many others are more educated than me. So many others have a neater past than me. You said "No. For my grace is sufficient for you. You are made perfect in weakness. I do not call the equipped, I equip the called." So here I am. Broken, unequipped, fragile me all for the glory of God. I will share about our awesome Father, who created the heavens and the earth, how He restores the broken, how He lavishes His love on us and how He is always faithful.

FIFTY-ONE

January 2019
Dear Jesus,

My recent visit to the rheumatologist was a far cry from what I thought it was going to be. This is the understatement of the year. Usually when I think I know what You are doing in my life in a certain situation, it never is the outcome that I anticipated. Why? Because You always do immeasurably more than we ask or imagine. I had a name pegged to my illness. I had myself feeling great and full of energy. I had me viewing my illness in the rearview mirror. What actually happened? Nothing. Nada. Zilch.

My hope was in You, Jesus. My hope was larger than life and I believed I was going to get my answers...all the way up to the lingering last test result. I just knew it was going to be positive for some chromosomal defect and the medical professionals were going to be able to tell me how to manage my illness so that I would eventually feel better. My last test result came back normal. Just like I had dreaded. I wondered why You took me through all of this for just another let down. It was not what I wanted to hear. Then I remembered something that happened the first day I met the rheumatologist. We went over my lengthy list of strange illnesses over the years and his ears perked up over a certain period of time in my early twenties. Immediately he diagnosed an illness that I had twenty years ago. I skimmed over it because I was looking ahead to where I thought You were taking me. Okay, can I cut to the chase? I am sorry for my lack of faith. I am a lost, stubborn, know-it-all sheep who desperately needs a Shepherd.

Sitting in the room I described a part of my life I tucked neatly away. I was around the age of twenty. I was working, nannying, and going to college for early childhood education. One day I had a fever. The next day I had a fever. It went on for a year of my life. I quit my job. I quit nannying and I quit college. I stayed isolated in my mom's house with all my test results pointing to normal. Friends tired of hearing my same old story and stopped coming around. It was a very lonely time for me personally. The medical staff even questioned my illness. They thought I was depressed. A year after being sick, an Ear, Nose and Throat specialist took out my tonsils. It was a last-ditch effort, however, miraculously it worked. Once my tonsils were removed, the fevers stopped and my life resumed. I started a new job and buried that part of my life. In one visit with me, the rheumatologist matter-of-factly stated what I had at that time. He put a name on it. The end. Simply just like that. One year of suffering, twenty years of burying and it was exposed and known.

I missed the beauty of this redeemed time because my eyes were off target. My eyes were on me and what I thought You were doing in my life instead of walking daily with You and allowing Your truth to heal and free me from a hard, life-altering stage of my life. I wonder how many times we miss the boat. Our eyes are looking past our circumstances, or they are looking in the rear-view mirror instead of focusing in the here and now. I almost, almost missed this beautiful jewel You placed before me. You, Lord, know everything about us. You know the plans You have for us. You know how to orchestrate everything in creation to make this happen for us. You always do immeasurably more than we ask or imagine because You are God. You are all authority and power. Again, I am reminded to sit down. Slow down. Simplify and listen quietly to Your voice today.

FIFTY-TWO

January 7, 2019
Dear Jesus,

Somewhere along the way I fell in love with vintage and You. I am a vintage-faith girl. Vintage-faith reveals a repaired, restored life. When we started building our third new house, I started finding my own way. I learned what I like and what I do not like. When I was newly married, I did not care about my likes. I wanted what everyone else wanted. I went through the store making my registry list based on new fads, friends, and other's opinions. Somewhere along the way I grew up. We never planned on building three houses, but life happened. We built our second house in an area where we could have more land, a smaller school, and I could stay home and raise our children. We built our third house out of dire necessity for peace, safety, and privacy. Somewhere in the middle of the mess, I grew up. I found You as my deepest source of peace.

I began shopping to furnish our new non-traditional house. I found I love the old pieces. The pieces which held a history and had character. The pieces that were unique. I love the rough edges of old pieces of furniture. I love the chipped areas. I love the different colors and the distinct lines. I love breaking the rules and using old pieces for something different than their intended purpose. I love the pieces that were almost unusable and then transformed by a light, patient touch. Somehow, someway the silver frames, classic couches, and ordinary dressers were not my style. My new home did not look like everyone else's house anymore. It looked unique. One of a kind. Mine. I wonder if that is how each one of us looks to You?

I have gathered quite a few nametags through the years. For a while, I let some of these nametags define me. Two of the nametags I have carried with me the longest are liar and quitter. Instead of being okay with who I was and what my choices were, I tended to lie or hide. Instead of following through on things when the going got tough, I tended to retreat or quit. I followed this cycle for years. I never thought I would be able to get off the vicious wheel of lies I believed. I did not believe I was worthy of a better name. I did not believe I could be something or someone who was perfect in her own skin. And then I met You.

Somewhere along the way I got tired. I knew I could not do this life alone. I did not want to do this life alone. I began to pray. Pray fervently. I began to study Your word. I began to meet with others who believed in You. I began to make good choices. I began to step out of my comfort zone. I began to become the true me when I surrendered my life to You, Jesus. Did this happen overnight? Not at all. To be truthful the process has been much slower than I would have liked, but the process has revealed a restored life which looks more like You every day. You sand down my rough edges. You leave some of my chipped areas and define other areas leaving distinct lines. You have taken this old piece and fulfilled Your purpose for me. I am vintage faith. A life transformed by a light, patient touch.

Those old nametags? They have no place around my neck. They do not define me. You are the one who defines me, Jesus. You are the one who names me. You call me chosen (1 Pet. 2:9), loved (John 3:16), forgiven (Isa. 1:18), cherished (Jer. 31:3), Yours (Eph. 1:5).

FIFTY-THREE

January 8, 2019
Dear Jesus,

I have a problem. A couple years ago I would have said I do not have this problem anymore. I would have sworn my life on it! *But!* It is not true. I have a problem with people pleasing. I thought I had come a long way since becoming a mother. I started putting my children and their needs first, even if it was not mainstream. I no longer catered to people's times, dates, and requirements if it was not in the best interest of my family. Of course, I love spending time with friends and family, but time just looked a little different than it used to. I thought I was perfectly okay with people disagreeing with me if I thought I was doing what You would want me to do. Well, I think You are going to have to do a little more refining in me in this area.

Thoughts. Thoughts consume and control. Thoughts fluctuate. Are never stable. I am an overthinker and I am a people pleaser. I think a lot of people fall into this category and waste too much energy on worrying about how others perceive them. I went to an extra-curricular event recently. The event is new to me and I am learning what this looks like. What I have noticed is when people's children are done for the day, the parents stay and watch the other teammates finish their day. Some of the days are long. Seriously, for me, as much as I love it, they are all long days.

This Saturday at the event, my daughter was not feeling well. She handled the day well, but by the end of the day, she had had it. Tears were welling in her eyes and her headache was unbearable. I decided to pack up and leave. My son was done, but not all the participants had completed their day. I felt shame leaving. I felt judgment. I wondered what the other parents were saying about me. Many of the parent's children had finished hours before and they were still there. Other spectators without any children participating came and watched and stayed until all the students had finished.

The old lies started to creep into my mind. You always quit. You could have stayed. You are selfish. I wanted more than anything to plead my case. I wanted to tell everyone there that my daughter was sick. I rationalized what I thought You would say. Only care what I think. You are making the best decision you know how to make in the best interest of your daughter. They probably are not thinking anything about you. But deep down, I know what the problem is. I want to fit in. I want them to accept me and like me. I cannot stand the thought of others thinking poorly of me. It is not only this scenario, but I see so many people struggling with these situations as well.

- Everyone in my Christian community participates in youth group, AWANA, or Sunday school, but it does not make sense for my family. Do I send my children anyway? Do others?

- Someone asks if I can take care of their children, but due to certain circumstances I do not want to or am unable. Do I do it anyway? Do others?

- Someone asks me to squeeze in a job for them when it is impossible with my already crammed schedule. Do I do it anyway? Do others?

- I cancel an appointment with a friend because of a time conflict and reschedule at a later time with someone else. Do I feel guilty? Do others?

- I am asked to volunteer on a committee to better the community, but I decline because I do not want to or do not have the time. Do I do it anyway? Do others?

- I am asked to use my skills to build something for a cause I believe in but due to time, I am unable. Do I do it anyway?

Do others?

- I am asked to host an event for a friend but do not want to. Do I do it anyway? Do others?
- I feel pressured between public school, private school, or homeschooling. Do I do what all my friends are doing because I feel like I should because if it is the best decision for them it must be for my family as well? Do others?
- I am pressured to make decisions for my children based on other's criteria like cell phone usage, age to date, foods to eat, etc. Are others?

Jesus, this type of thinking is exhausting. Maybe no one is conflicted with these same thoughts, but maybe, just maybe I have some company in this. When I move against the mainstream, I may not be popular. It may be a struggle. My thoughts *do* try to consume me. For me, when my thoughts cripple me, I need to get back to my roots. My roots which are deeply planted in the Word of God will tell me the truth. "So then, just as you received Christ Jesus as Lord, continue to live Your lives in him, rooted and built up in him, strengthened in the faith as you were taught, and overflowing with thankfulness" (Col. 2:7).

I need to know that if I am living in truth, following You and doing the best I know how to do that is enough no matter what anyone else thinks. My relationship with You is mine. It is not the same as anyone else's. What is right for me may not be right for others. What is right for them may not be right for me. Peter says it this way, "I now realize how true it is that God does not show favoritism but accepts from every nation the one who fears him and does what is right. (Acts 10: 34–35) I wonder how many of us waste time and energy worrying about such trivial matters. Again, I will continue to walk in love and roots, so I can be set free from this people pleasing once and for all.

The older I get I realize I cannot rely on humans for approval.

We as people have different opinions, are raised with different circumstances and all have different ideas. What I want my life to look like is grace, love, and truth. I think if all of people worried more about what the King of kings thought about us, we would not have time to focus on if a mom stays in the stands the whole time, or this overthinking mom would not have time presuming people were always thinking the worst of her. I do not want to fluctuate with my feelings and thoughts any longer. I want to be steady and sure. I no longer want to be an immature Christ follower who is tossed back and forth on mere circumstances. I want to keep my focus on You and Your word and what You say about me. You say I am Yours (Isa. 43:1), enough (1 Pet. 2:9) and made perfect in Your image (Gen. 1:27). My roots have just given me wings. Wings to sore on the heights. My roots have set me free.

> A farmer went out to sow his seed. As he was scattering the seed, some fell along the path, and the birds came and ate it up. Some fell on rocky places, where it did not have much soil. It sprang up quickly because the soil was shallow. But when the sun came up, the plants were scorched, and they withered because they had no root. Other seed fell among thorns, which grew up and choked the plants. Still other seed fell on good soil, where it produced a crop
> Matthew 13:3–8

FIFTY-FOUR

January 18, 2019
Dear Jesus,

You know that girl that struts in a room, holds her head high, speaks boldly and shines radiantly? That is not me.

You know that girl who shamelessly walks across the beach in her swimsuit posing for all the pictures with the ocean in the background? That is not me.

You know that girl who posts all the selfies for everyone to see her beauty? That is not me.

You have just exposed something in me. It has always been there in different forms, but it has just come to light in a new way. I would rather be hidden than for anyone to see the real me. It hit me out of nowhere. Right now. The light just went on and the real problem was exposed plain as day. I am self-critical and lack confidence and any kind of inner compassion. I am the girl who is always comparing my worth to others. Always wondering what others are thinking of me. Always wishing my academics, career, body, and looks were something different.

You have slowly been revealing this to me over time, but the bomb was dropped on me today. After a broken relationship, I began writing with Your word to heal. Over time, friends, family members, and acquaintances began asking for my writings or asking if they could pass them on to others in need. I was thrilled that You were using my pain for a greater purpose. As my writing continued, my journey has as well. I attended a Christian writing conference, shared my testimony in groups of people, finally joined social media, and now started a new blog. This broken me is becoming something new. Someone I hardly recognize. I prefer my life to be private and hate the thought of being exposed publicly, but that is exactly where You are leading me. Every time I share a writing, take a microphone, or post something publicly, I feel ill. My mind races. My thoughts too. What has been revealed to me has come in other forms as well. Yesterday I received a photo of myself in my swimsuit on vacation. The thoughts I had of myself were not good. I felt complete dread thinking someone else would see this picture. I immediately deleted the photo hoping I could erase it from my mind and pretend it never existed. I cried with this new revelation. I am ashamed of me. If I feel this way, surely other women feel this way? My family members? Friends? Loved ones? My daughter? My beautiful daughter. Does she feel this way now? Will she ever? The real me has been hidden in plain sight.

I want to stomp out this lie that I am not good enough. I want to take this weak, fragile soul and infuse it with strength. I want to walk in truth boldly and confidently. I want to say I am worthy. I am enough. Chosen and created. I want to shout it from the rooftops. Not for me, but for all people. I do not want to believe the lies anymore that say I am not pretty enough, thin enough, smart enough. That I have not performed enough, produced enough, achieved enough. I want to take captive every thought and make it obedient to Christ (2 Cor. 10:5). I want to unveil the real me. The fearfully and wonderfully made me (Ps. 139:14). The chosen me (1 Pet. 2:9). The bought at a price me (1 Cor. 6:20). The one and only me (Jer. 1:5).

Why are You revealing this to me? Why are You restoring me? I believe it is simple. I asked. I sit with You. I spend time with You. I read Your word and ask unending questions. I wrestle with You. Constantly. Why? I do this because I want more than this broken world has to offer. I do this because I want to be transformed, healed, and whole. I know that because of sin I can never be whole apart from You. I can never be at rest. Through trials and struggles, my brokenness—this world's brokenness—becomes more and more visible. This is what You offer all people. A restored life. A whole life. A life which reveals a newer and stronger person! A life free of comparison. A life free of idolatry. A life free of coveting. A life full of peace and assurance.

FIFTY-FIVE

January 2019
Dear Jesus,

Will I feel naked forever? Will my cheeks ever turn back to their normal color? How long will my mind race? How long will I question my words? How long must I wrestle with my thoughts? How long will I care how others perceive me? Is it normal to search who likes my post? If people do not like your post does that mean they do not like you? Oh boy, my mind is a battlefield. Am I the only one? Something tells me many other people deal with this. Everyone desires to be liked and loved.

My church took a break after the many Christmas services and had a day of rest and worship from home last Sunday. My family visited a local church near our home. A church we love to attend. Brandon had to work early that morning to get ahead before we leave on vacation next week. I was alone at home with our kids and getting ready for church was going to be my task for the morning. A mighty big task I might add. Christmas vacation, no schedule, too many sweets, and an exhaustive schedule was not going to work in my favor. I woke the children maybe ten times and then finally got into the car and waited for the grumbling tribe to enter. We drove to the church in silence. A quiet thought emerged. *If someone asks you to share a testimony this morning, you need to do it.* Where did that thought come from? Why? Oh, why? My thoughts wandered as we pulled up to the big white work truck. Brandon jumped in and we parked nearby the red brick building.

We settled into our seats and were greeted by a few friendly faces. The worship began, followed by a prayer, and then the pastor

191

walked up to the microphone. He introduced a few people who were being baptized and then he asked for anyone who would be willing to share a pain-filled personal testimony. I began to sweat. When it was time, I rose. Scared. A few others rose too. I sat and waited my turn. When it was time, I took the microphone. I introduced myself, shared a personal, painful loss, shared my brokenness, and then read a poem I wrote about coming to realize that nothing satisfies but Jesus alone. The poem is about You doing the work in our lives and about letting go and letting You do Your work. When I looked up from the microphone, there were many tears in the audience. There were tears on my face too. I wondered why for a minute. The delivery was not pretty. I choked out the words. I cried and fumbled with the microphone and my phone. Then I remembered people do not need perfect, they need real. I can do real. Only by Your grace.

As I took my seat, I was met with a fist bump. As the sermon concluded I was met by many people as I exited. People thanked me for my testimony, but one woman thanked me for obeying the Spirit because she felt it was a message the church desperately needed to hear that morning. Praise You, Jesus. That evening as I laid down in bed, I received a message from the pastor thanking me for my testimony and told me it affected many people in the church that day. For a minute I felt good for obeying You. At peace. Settled. When I woke in the morning, I had another email from the pastor. A young woman contacted him telling him how much she was affected by my testimony and my poem. She asked for my contact information. This young woman then messaged me. She lavished grace on me, and I felt good that You used me to encourage her, but then she asked me for a copy of my writing. I told her I would pray about it. Early on as I began to write, my mentor and I decided not to print out and share my writings. I want to use them to encourage others, but I want to wait for Your perfect timing. I prayed about this and I finally decided to do something unthinkable. I posted my writing on Facebook. The good, peaceful, and settled feeling left the building.

I thought I had jumped the week prior just joining social media. Then I thought I jumped by posting. Then I thought I jumped by being transparent. Well, I just jumped off the cliff. I do not think I have landed yet. When I asked You to use me, I failed to remember I need to be willing to follow wherever You take me. I am still not comfortable with it at all. I feel naked. Unequipped. Exposed. Unnatural. Raw. Judged. I wonder if I will ever feel natural again. This is what I do know. You are worth it. I said goodbye to complacency a long time ago and I have had the most beautiful views from Your perspective. As believers, we are all called to share You in our own special way using the gifts, You gave us. You are faithful. You will finish what You started in me. You will clothe us with Your love and will equip those You have called. You will use our transparency and willingness to serve to help others.

What good would it do if I were a natural writer and speaker? What good would it do if I were naturally outgoing and loved to be the center of attention? How would that show Your power and majesty? It would not. Plain and simple. When I choose to follow You, it displays Your glory. It exposes Your supernatural power working through me.

FIFTY-SIX

January 22, 2019
Dear Jesus,

I do not belong on a pedestal. Leaders do not belong on a pedestal. Followers of Jesus do not belong on a pedestal. "For all have sinned and fall short of the glory of God" (Rom. 3:23).

Why do people put Christians on a pedestal? If people spend an hour with me, a day with me, or if they came into my house and visited with me, they would see I am far from perfect. I make mistakes hourly, daily, constantly. If people are not aware of them verbally, then they just need to step into my thoughts or view my actions. If I ever proclaim to be perfect, please call me out on it. I would love to be perfect and blameless. I would love to walk in perfect step with You who was tempted in every way without sin, but it is not going to happen. *Ever.* I will continue to grow and look more like You, but I will never be perfect.

A few years ago, I had an argument with someone I love. The argument turned ugly. I was hurt beyond belief and crushed in my spirit. I called a friend and told her what had happened. I was completely transparent and vulnerable with her. I gave her details I would have preferred to keep to myself, but I was desperate for prayer. So, I purged the whole gory story. I explained that I had been praying about it, but I was so bitter and struggling with my actions toward the individual. I coveted her prayer in this area. I knew I was sinning in my thoughts and actions and I was repenting to God for it. I asked my friend to hold me up in prayer. A few days later, there was a get together with a few families. My friend I confided in and the person I had the argument with were both present. The next day, I received a call from my friend, and she pointed out three areas in how I sinned against this person at the gathering. I gasped. I cried. The knife penetrated deep into my soul. I did not belong on that pedestal.

A year ago, a close friend of mine came to me and asked me to hold her accountable in an area she was struggling. I was happy to help her and honored she asked. I also was proud of her for acknowledging her weakness and vulnerably asking for help. Soon after, my dear friend stopped calling. She stopped responding to my messages. I knew something was wrong and finally, I asked her point blank if I had done something wrong. She messaged me and asked for my forgiveness because she failed in the area she was struggling. Her message was so transparent, and I knew she was crushed and ashamed of her weakness. I remember telling her that Jesus had already forgiven her and that she needed to forgive herself.

Honestly, I thought nothing differently of my sweet Jesus-following friend, but time went on and her friendship disappeared from my life. I was crushed and felt a deep loss because I truly treasured her. A few months later, I received grand news from her in the mail. I could not be happy though. I kept looking at the piece of mail and I was feeling complete unrest. I knew what I had to do. I picked up the phone scared and told the truth. I told her I was struggling being happy for her. I called her out on her abandonment of our friendship. I told her the enemy would love nothing more than for us to hide in our shame, but when we bring it out into the open, we are healed. You took this moment to cleanse both of us, bringing our struggle into the light. I did not belong on that pedestal.

A few years ago, I went to a teacher in confidence. I came frail and broken. I had never done anything like this before, but I was desperate. I went unannounced and asked for a small group of people to pray for me and a volatile situation I was in. I left feeling less alone. I shared a few unrelated parting words and left. A couple hours later, an email was sent out. My few unrelated words were mass produced in an email. When I came for prayer, it was one of the worst days I had ever experienced and when the email went out it made me feel like works were more important than love. That leader did not belong on that pedestal.

Friends, teachers, loved ones, and family members all let us down. We are all doing the best we can on this journey, and we are all sinners. When I told my friend the areas where I was struggling, I did not need her to point out the areas I had failed in. I already knew I was failing. I was already repenting about it and praying about it. I needed love, support, and grace. When my friend came and asked me to keep her on the straight and narrow, I was happy to do so in love and grace. When she failed, she hid and put me on a pedestal where I did not belong. When my teacher let me down, I had put him on a pedestal thinking he would never make a mistake. You are the only one who knew no sin.

Jesus, I have learned Christians are not holier than thou. All one needs to do is step into a church and they will see this to be true. Christians are just people who love Jesus and *repent*. "It is not the healthy who need a doctor, but the sick. I have not come to call the righteous, but sinners to repentance" (Mark 2:17).

FIFTY-SEVEN

January 27, 2019
Dear Jesus,

It had been a few weeks since I found the yellow square paper on my front doorstep. The piece of paper that did not belong there. The piece of paper written in lies. The action that stated violation all over it. The piece of paper that left me bent over gasping for air on my gravel drive. Today was a new day. It was hot outside and late afternoon. The air was so heavy you could almost see it. My four children piled into the car ready to get their hair cut. We backed out of the garage and watched the door close as we rounded the corner down the drive. Since the paper showed up, there was something different about me. I held a tense demeanor always looking over my shoulder and lines on my forehead were always crunched in terse lines. The pose held as I drove the short drive to town. We parked on the street next to the red brick lined buildings and stepped into the musty shop. One at a time, my children stepped forward and took a seat on the vinyl swivel chairs. Three of my children stepped down and asked if they could cross the street over to the gas station to get a sucker. This new apprehensive me paused and then hesitantly nodded my head yes. I turned in my seat to watch my children cross the street. The kids were soon in the gas station out of sight and I suddenly had a wave of nausea. My children bounced back across the street moments later and pulled the heavy door open as the bell chimed. A smile reappeared on my face, but the ill feeling remained. As we headed back to the vehicle, we saw someone we recognized, and the children's looks begged me to walk past for fear of a lengthy conversation. I stopped and we visited. The children's looks were right again as we headed home much later.

The red house came into view and the white garage door started to rise. The sun was shining in an awkward way and my eyes drifted to the back of the 1979 Malibu. The back window was shattered with glass littering the back seat with one puncture hole. The bent over, gasping posture returned and I knew. I was violated. My thoughts ran rampant in my mind. Then I remembered my ill state in the hair salon and the detoured time. If we would have left promptly would we have found the perpetrator in my garage? On my driveway? I remember the police call, the whispers, my scared children and searching for evidence. I then I remember the scenarios, the discussion, the unbelief, and the explanations. But I knew the truth. That icky feeling never lies.

Today I was sitting in church listening to a message on sexual violation. My mind drifted to these two instances and then while I was tossing over these memories, another one appeared in my mind. It is jumbled and not completely accurate, but it happened all the same. Multiple days may be in the same frame, but one thing is for sure, someone chased us down, banged on our house, and tried to climb in through the window. Over a period of a year this scenario unfolds. I am lying on a king size mattress on the floor in my new unfamiliar space. My sister is sleeping next to me, but I have never felt so alone in my life. I hear banging downstairs. I hear loud voices wrestling. I feel panicked inside. Tears soaked the sheets underneath me and I fear I will drown in the tears. For the first time in my life I remember crying out to You, Jesus. I do not remember the words I used, but I remember an endless stream of words. I was violated. What these three offenses have in common is the perpetrator is the same.

The person violating me was someone I loved and someone who had authority over me. I was not violated sexually, but violated still. I trusted this person and in all three instances it created deep grief and confusion inside of me. The difference between the situations is in the first two I listed I was a grown woman, wife, and mother, but in the last description I was a nine-year-old child. Still. They felt the same in my mind. I felt alone and scared. Afraid to share and if I did share it was brushed under the rug or an argument ensued. Everyone in my life became bystanders. They witnessed it, processed it, and handled it separate from me. In my lonely, fearful state, I found in all situations something similar. Jesus was enough. When no one understood my pain, You did. When no one could talk about it, You could. When everyone had had enough, You remained. "The Lord is close to the brokenhearted and saves those who are crushed in spirit" (Ps. 34:18).

What I have learned through these painful experiences is the people you think will be there for you may not be. The people you think will protect you might not be able to. What I have learned is many people do not know how to handle pain and trauma; and therefore end up doing nothing. I am not judging my loved ones that did not know how to support me. What I am saying is You are never a bystander. You are close to the brokenhearted and You are more than enough to support me in my time of need. I want to take what I have learned and experienced and apply it to my life and those around me. I will learn to follow Your footsteps and learn to do right; seek justice. Defend the oppressed. Take up the cause of the fatherless; plead the case of the widow (Isa. 1:17). I choose to follow in Your footsteps. Even when it hurts. Even when it does not make sense. Even when it is uncomfortable. In one word. Love. I will learn to love as You have loved me.

FIFTY-EIGHT

February 8, 2019
Dear Jesus,

I hear You. I do not know why or how, but I do. Something has shifted. Your words have changed from: *hang on, persevere, keep going to you made it, it is raining blessings, well done.* My circumstances have not changed, but I have learned to listen to Your voice and trust it anyway. Six years ago, I heard You speak. It was loud. Not in volume, but in constant circumstances all pointing in the same direction. The direction of freedom and it all started with a rainbow and a promise.

God said, "This is the sign of the promise I am giving to you and every living being that is with you for generations to come. I will put my rainbow in the clouds to be a sign of my promise to the earth" (Gen. 9:12–13).

Icicles covered the branches as I made my way down the curvy, cracked blacktop. The winter had been hard on the pavement this year. Looking out my window I was mesmerized by the light and the glistening of the frost covered branches. Moving further down the road, the frosted branches now looked like icicles. The view was pristine like the made-up Ice World on Nintendo and then I looked up. The round, bright sun was encircled with a rainbow. On each end you could see the colors, but the middle was faint, almost translucent. You could make the shape out and I did what no one should ever do. I smiled and reached for my phone to try and capture this miraculous sight. I was handling the curves of the road, manipulating the ice chunks on the uneven pavement, and holding the camera just so, as to miss the rearview mirror. The picture is less than perfect, but I captured the rainbow none the less. I made it to my destination and went into my appointment thinking about the last time I saw a rainbow like that. A smile re-appeared on my face.

I sat rocking in my blue rocking recliner reading some verses off my Instagram feed when I arrived home. One of the first verses I came across was Zephaniah 3:17: "The Lord your God is with you, the Mighty Warrior who saves. He will take great delight in you; in his love he will no longer rebuke you but will rejoice over you with singing." Again, my thoughts drifted to six years ago when I saw that beautiful rainbow, heard You tell me my struggle was over, and then read the words scripted out in Zephaniah. I sat pondering Your miraculous ways when a message appeared on my phone. A friend of mine had just been to a concert and thought of me and a song she sang about rainbows.

Oh. My. Goodness. I am overwhelmed by Your goodness and mercy. Your timing. Your miraculous ways. Your love that surrounds me with singing. You speak loud and clear and You use whatever and whoever You choose to make Your message known. This morning I am in awe of the creator of heaven and earth. I will praise Your holy name.

Give praise to the Lord, proclaim his name; make known among the nations what he has done. Sing to him, sing praise to him; tell of all his wonderful acts. Glory in his holy name; let the hearts of those who seek the Lord rejoice. Look to the Lord and his strength; seek his face always.

Psalm 105:1–4

Knowledge is good, studying is good, but faith is even better. Now faith is confidence in what we hope for and assurance about what we do not see. This is what the ancients were commended for. (Heb. 11:1–2) My faith has given me sight. A view of You, Your ways, Your love, care, and direction. It cannot be explained, written about, or studied. It is an experience you can only encounter when you have a personal relationship with You, Jesus. It leaves my mouth open, my knees on the floor, and my hands raised in holy wonder.

FIFTY-NINE

February 22, 2019
Dear Jesus,

It was a snowy afternoon and I made my way around the last curve leading to my hidden driveway. A doe lay hidden behind the scraggly fence behind my mailbox. Ice covered my driveway while icicles dangled off the roof edge and the snow in my front field glistened with untouched snow. The sight was breathtaking, but something in view was fractured. There are three mailboxes across the street from my property. Two neighbors' mailboxes and ours. One mailbox was untouched, standing tall. One mailbox was severed at the root, lying lifeless on the ground. My mailbox was battered, dented, and a little crooked. A few days have passed since this image, but my life has collided with this image of the mailboxes.

It all started with brokenness. Then pain birthed a passion and desire deep in the center of my core. A passion to follow You with all my heart and soul. I was hungry for You, Jesus, and the word of God. I could not get enough of You. Watching You work in the tiniest details of my life. Putting broken pieces back together, restoring my life, and watching You fulfill the purpose You placed on my life. The journey is magnificent, painful, and challenging. As I began devouring all You have to offer, my life began falling apart. My marriage became strained and parenting became a struggle. Why is following You, Jesus, and serving You so hard? I have a glimpse of the plans You have for me and I am running all out to fulfill this purpose. I see You move in the components of my life and I know You are speaking to me, breathing life into me and I continue to run this race marked out for me. My relationships continue to struggle and I am feeling just like my mailbox: battered, dented, and crooked. How can there be such chaos in my home? All the accusations and fighting feels as if it is all directed at me. I want peace here. I want love here. I want joy here. I want to be unified under this roof. I see such division. I am following You, serving, praying, and reading Your Word. It feels as if I am the only one doing the uncomfortable and the hard. Why is everything coming against me? Why don't others see You in me? Why aren't You beautiful in me?

My frayed heart is sagging. I have become weary in doing good. In a last-ditch effort, I muster a little faith and strength and humbly make a phone call. I sat on a dark leather couch adjacent to help. Tears trickled down my cheeks as I asked aloud, "Why isn't Jesus attractive in me?" I am crumbling in my own house. A story followed and peace steadied itself in my soul. I heard three things in this visit. One, my family is a gift from God, and You gave me my family first to love, serve, treasure, and enjoy. Two, I can fulfill my calling without deserting my husband and my children. Three, rest. Rest in Christ. You are the one doing the work and fulfilling the plans You have for me. You will do the leading and completing the work of Your hands. These three principles were later reiterated to me by two different people, at two separate times and by two people who do not even know each other. You, Jesus, can teach by the power of Your Spirit. Three people conveyed Your message loud and clear. "You, Kari, have been off-roading. Cease striving and know that I am God" (Ps. 46:10 NASB).

As these truths settled in my mind a song came to mind. I began to hum,

In Christ alone my hope is found, He is my light, my strength, my song, this Cornerstone, this solid ground, firm through the fiercest drought and storm, what heights of love, what depths of peace, when fears are stilled, when strivings cease, my Comforter, my All in All, here in the love of Christ I stand.

"In Christ Alone"

Oh, Lord have mercy on me. I have taken over the wheel. I have been led astray. Easily. Sneakily. What looked so good. So godly. So Christian. I wonder how many others are off-roading as I type. I wonder if anyone else has a blind spot? My story started beautifully. It started with a calling and a purpose from You, but somewhere along the way control took over Your leading. It is so easy to veer off course when I am not in constant communication with You, reading Your word and resting in You. I had a blind spot and it took me away from my family and created division in my marriage and my home. All this time I have been chasing You, Jesus, and leaving my family behind. All along I thought Brandon and my children were not doing their part, but really it was me.

You know what I did? I came home. I rested. I played some Yahtzee with one of my favorite teens. I sat and colored some pictures with the prettiest little girl I know. I played outside while my children built a snowman. I baked some favorite treats for my boys. I spent an evening with my family watching a sporting event that we love. I turned off Facebook. I put other apps to bed. Did I turn You off completely? Did I forgo my calling? Absolutely not! I still read Your word. I still pray. I still worship. I am still running the race marked out for me. The only difference is I stopped striving. You are leading and I am following. And You know what happened, Jesus? I am not frazzled and I am not weary. My family is not divided and all I had to do was stand in Your love.

SIXTY

March 11, 2019
Dear Jesus,

Before my final test result was read from the rheumatology department, I was on the phone discussing the final stage of our upcoming vacation. When we were finished discussing business, I asked a personal question. The rheumatologist was leaning toward an autoimmune disorder and I had heard my friend had experience in this area. I did not pry and not many details were given, but she shared with me someone who had helped her medically. She told me all the things I did not want to hear. With the right diet, right supplements, and stress relief I believe you can get better. No disrespect to this woman, but hog wash. Bologna. No, thank you, ma'am. I had been there. Done that. I have exercised. I have been a runner, done CrossFit, aerobics, walked for days. I have tried diets. I have gone paleo, Atkins, Whole 30, you name it. I have tried essential oils, herbs, vitamins, and teas. I have gotten massages, gone to the chiropractor, had injections. Some of these things have helped me maintain my life, but mostly what I have gotten is flares including rashes, exhaustion, weight gain, and more exhaustion.

I have been at war. Searching, longing, fighting for my health my whole life. I want nothing more than to feel good, strong, and whole physically. I thought the rheumatologist was going to be my knight in shining armor; the man who would miraculously diagnose me and set me high upon the rock whole. When my final test result came back normal, I catapulted from my visionary high rock to the ground. Friends and loved ones were just as discouraged as I. They said all the things I felt. Things like, he said he would not give up

209

easily. He said he would fight for an answer. Go back and demand more testing, more answers. But. I knew. My fighting was over. I needed someone else to fight my battle. This battle is not mine.

I prayed on my way home after leaving my girlfriend's house. Please, Lord. I am done fighting. Please tell me what to do. Please tell me what foods to eat and what exercise to do. I believe You want to heal me. Show me the way. I want to be whole physically, emotionally, spiritually, and mentally. Set me high upon the rock for Your glory. You are the Physician. Amen.

The next morning, I received a phone call. Our flight schedule changed for our vacation and our agent called to inform me. When we were finished discussing details, she asked me how I was feeling. I expressed my frustration and told her my test results were all normal, but I was still feeling terrible. She then expressed how much the woman she had told me about had helped her when she was ill. She did not tell me to go. She did not tell me to do anything. She just shared what had helped her. I was still resistant, and I did not want to go. I did not understand why, and I did not understand how. I only knew I had stepped aside, and I gave You the wheel. I hesitantly asked for the woman's name and she gave it to me. I scheduled my first appointment with a kinesiologist.

You never do what I think You will do. I have come to understand that You are not just mysterious, but faithful and sovereign. You are full of mercy and grace. All-knowing. Praise Your holy name. I heard You clearly a few years ago state that you are restoring me. Restoring my life and not just part of it, but all of it. You are restoring my health. I believe You, Jesus. I trust You and know You will do immeasurably more than I ask or imagine. If I could just get out of the way and let You work. Well, that is what I am doing now. I consciously remind myself daily to let You work. Let You heal. Let You lead. I sit with You and I listen to You and obey where You take me.

I filled out my paperwork at my first appointment. I tried to include everything I could think of. Her demeanor was undisturbed, joyful, and optimistic. When I shared that my medical records look like an autoimmune disorder, she shook her head in disbelief. She believed I just needed the right supplements to heal my organs naturally. She examined me and I came home with a bag of supplements and a dietary plan just for me. A direct answer to prayer. I was tired of trying all different things not knowing what I needed. All the things I had tried in the past were not bad and some even helped me, but none were tailored just for me. I needed someone to tell me exactly how to feed my body and this is what I asked my heavenly Father for. I was spent and ready for You to do the battling for me. When I asked, You faithfully directed me to my solid Rock. You are the one who set me there high and whole. I am whole because You are my source. I am not perfect yet, but gradually making progress. My symptoms are insignificant, my joints are not sore, I am less tired, my low blood sugar disappeared, the rashes are gone, and so are the flares and migraines. I am continuing to walk with You and take my part in my healing journey. As far as making plans and trying to figure out the steps You have prepared for me? I have decided to let You be.

"The Lord will fight for you; you need only to be still" (Ex. 14:14).

SIXTY-ONE

March 26, 2019
Dear Jesus,

I fell into bed and melted into the white flannel sheets as I drifted to sleep easily. A few hours later I awoke to headlights peeking through my transparent ivory curtains. My eyes were blurry. I rubbed them gently as I peered out the window. My mind wandered through the evening and I remembered our house guest had been picked up and Brandon and Lukas had arrived hours before. I slowly emerged through the slight walkway. The house was black, and I felt hidden behind my front door and the welcoming wreath covering most of the glass window. I crouched low beneath the wreath to see who it was. I saw a dark vehicle and just outside the door I saw denim and the hem of a dark green t-shirt. I saw a large hand emerge from the jean pocket and a piece of yellow paper drop. Seconds later I heard a flick as the Post-it was consumed by fire drifting to the edge of my house. As I gasped, I breathed in the most familiar scent. I sat up suddenly with sweat beading on my forehead. I cried aloud, Jesus.

This dream was a few nights ago. I am grateful it was only a dream, but honestly it has left me on edge. I was thinking about it this morning as I jumped my hundredth rope and headed out the door. I pulled up to the familiar coffee shop as I spied my mom's car across the street. We walked in together, bought our coffee, and found a table in the back where we would hold our weekly Bible study. Our last friend arrived, and conversation filled the richly scented air. After our first few sips of coffee were had, and we were caught up to speed on life in general, we headed to the private room in the back where we could watch our video of the week.

Sheila just began to speak and the words that left her mouth kicked me in the gut. Immediately tears spilled down my cheeks as her words resonated deep within my soul. Sheila Walsh spoke these words, "My dad died in a psychiatric hospital when he was thirty-four years old. And honestly, I think I had been running from that place and that legacy for most of my life. When someone would say to me, "Sheila, you remind me so much of your dad," I think they probably meant, "You sing like your dad," or "You have brown eyes like your dad," but what I heard in the darkest place of my heart was, "There is a flaw that runs deep in you just like your father and one day, no matter how fast you run, it will bring you down." Just like that. My heart was revealed in his presence.

Jesus, You have a way with people. A way no one can fathom. You see us fully. You know us. You know exactly what we need and exactly when we need it. You are the father of redemption. You are coming for us. Each one of us. Not for us, but for the glory of the Father. You are refining us. Restoring us. Redeeming us. For Your story. The story about a loving father who comes back for His kids so that one day we can live in glory with Him as it should be. You love us too much to leave us out of the garden forever. You came back for us. You sent Your son Jesus to die for us. To save us from our sin. In the process You mold us into the image of Christ until our work here on earth fulfills Your purpose. I needed this broken place in my soul restored today so that I can be healed and whole.

What You uncovered today was a fear I did not even know existed. A fear that one day I would turn out just like my dad; after all I have always thought I was a lot like him. But God. You revealed truth into the broken place of my heart. *Kari. You are my daughter. You may have similarities to your earthy father because you share genes, but you. You are unique. Fearfully and wonderfully made. And. You had a choice. We all have a choice. You chose me. You chose to walk in truth. You chose to come out of the darkness into my marvelous light.*

You made one choice. Then another and then another. Now all that is behind you are two sets of footprints where we walked together. Because. You had a will. And you chose.

I am thankful for Your grace. I am thankful that every time I choose to look up, You are right there waiting. I am thankful You know how to clean house. My house. I want You to continue to clear up the clutter. Clean up any and everything that is holding me back. I do not want to be stuck. During my faith-walk, I do not want my tires spinning spraying mud. I want to be consciously and consistently moving forward to be fruitful for Your kingdom.

"Be strong and courageous. Do not be terrified; do not be discouraged. For the Lord, your God will be with you wherever you go" (Josh. 1:9).

"THE VESSEL"

There is a rustling inside
Unsettled
Restless
Quaking
An imbalance
Fulfilling the Great Commission
Vs.
Private complacency
Oh Lord
How beautiful are the feet who bring good news?
Never let us be put to shame
Those who step out and stand out
Pour out your favor
Uphold us with your righteous right hand
I do not like this feeling
The feeling of the vessel being used
The cart is coming through
There is shaking and power coursing through the walls
Let it out
Oh Lord
Let it out
Let your kingdom come
Your will be done
So that everyone will know your name

SIXTY-TWO

April 11, 2019
Dear Jesus,

Faith. Faith requires something of you. It requires you to move. Step out. Even when you cannot see. Without faith steps your faith is not faith. It is just the same life as it was before you accepted Jesus as Your Lord and Savior. I need to be honest about something. I am a dreamer. A believer. I am a "go big or go home" kind of girl. I have taken a step out of my comfort zone believing something You put on my heart. I have felt deep in the depths of my soul that You have been writing my story for Your glory. I have believed that You are going to take my story to Your people who desperately need water for their thirsty soul. You see, during the last several years, I have been in the desert. In a dry and weary land where there is no water. I have said yes to truth and I have stepped off the crowded path. I have chosen to walk with You alone, trusting You to lead and teach me Your truths so that I could come back and share them with people who desperately need to hear it.

Can I tell You a secret? I do not like this one bit. Exposing my life, my pain, my brokenness for others to see, hear, and judge. I want to live privately and complacently, but You whispered something to me on the beautiful redemptive road. *Follow me.* So, I did. I have no idea where You are taking me. All I know is I said yes.

What I have found is the narrow road is not widely traveled. It is lonely. It sometimes looks strange to those who are watching. It sets you apart and makes you different and I have learned people like what is the same, not what is different. Following You takes guts. It takes someone who does not give up easily or is swayed by public opinion. I have found I not only fight against the current of popularity, but against my own flesh. My desires to be liked and normal and comfortable.

I have recently began sharing parts of my story to the public on social media. Again, I took another faith step trusting a dream I believe You put on my heart. The past two weeks have been an uphill trek. Sharing my story has allowed people I know and do not know to see me, my private pain, and my love for You, Jesus. I was anticipating sharing another form of social media would be challenging for me, but I never anticipated how challenging. I feel completely naked and exposed. Yesterday I hit a very deep low. I let my mind wander and fell prey to weakness.

The thought came in subtly. It had been lingering since my first post. Little doubts. Second thoughts. I began questioning the motives of my heart. The question appeared loud and clear: *Did You really desire me to share my story to a thirsty world or was it my personal desire to do something great with my name on it? Did I misunderstand the Lord's leading?* I melted into a pile of tears. My journey to impact others for You, Jesus, is over. I quit. I grieved letting it go. I grieved my weakness succumbing to failure. Thank You, Lord, for writing this story with me, but I think it is time I set the reins down. If it was only for my healing, then that is good enough for me. But. In one last attempt I sought You with clarity and with hungry fervor, devouring the word to see Your true heart in the matter.

Your answer? "I am not finished with you yet."

It all went downhill yesterday after my morning post. The post was on our identity and how it is found in Christ. I picked out the image and desired to inscribe the text, "You Are Seen." I fought with my thoughts and the words and ended up using the words, "You Are." I posted in flesh and not in the Spirit's leading. As I mulled over the chapter for today's posting, I became panicked. The title is: "You are chosen. You are set apart." I drowned in thoughts. *You do not know what you are talking about. You took His word out of context. You are not worthy to share His word. You are not qualified. You are not equipped to do this.* I flat out told You I was completely done posting my story. In my bossy state, I told You that You would have to make it abundantly clear if You wanted me to keep posting my story.

When I am at my weakest, humblest seeking out Your ways is when You speak up loud and clear. On my newsfeed on Facebook, a friend posted, "The God Who Sees." My mouth opened wide as I poured over scripture on how He is a God who sees and knows. My thoughts rushed back to my early morning post on, "You Are," knowing it should have read, "You Are Seen." Thank You, God, for Your special word. I trust it was for me. I too am seen and loved by you. Today, in my grieving, questioning state, You saw me. As I continued to wrestle with my thoughts, I logged back into my social media account and I continued to ponder whether I still was quitting. When in my feed the words read, *The God Who Sees,* a short film by Kathie Lee Gifford. The words again. I hear you so clearly. "I have not left you. You are weak, but I am strong. I see you." Just as the words rolled through my head, I see another post, "Set Apart and Chosen is now on social media!" My thoughts went straight to my story, my post, my big dream. I look up in holy wonder and whisper, *"Okay, Lord, okay."*

I know You are alive and active in my daily life. I love seeing You move and breathe and have Your being. You are faithful. You will answer. You will lead. You are a good, good Father. As far as my dream of sharing my story for Your glory. I will trust when I cannot see. I will continue to step off the crowded path and choose to trust You to lead and teach me Your truths. You can do anything. You can make a road in the desert. You can take a humble, meek servant and use them powerfully to serve Your kingdom.

"You, God, are my God, earnestly I seek you; I thirst for you, my whole being longs for you, in a dry and parched land where there is no water" (Ps. 63:1).

"But whoever drinks the water I give them will never thirst. Indeed, the water I give them will become in them a spring of water welling up to eternal life" (John 4:14).

SIXTY-THREE

April 29, 2019
Dear Jesus,

We started an adventure last year around this time. We began raising chickens. We brought home three chickens from school. Lukas sketched a coop and the boys and their dad built a stunning red-and-white chicken coop. I was resistant from the beginning, but realized raising chickens is a fun hobby for the whole family. Two of the chicks turned out to be roosters and one was a laying hen. We added six more layers and our family of chickens was complete, for this year anyway.

The first time we ran down to unlatch the tiny door leading to the laying box and found a green egg, we were hooked. It was like Christmas morning finding a little treasure laying on a bed of straw. Among the wonderful treasures there have also been heartache and trials. Most recently our challenge lies with the two roosters. Now one year old, they are showing off their masculinity and determining who is the king of the roost. From the beginning, one of the roosters, Apollo, has taken charge of the coop (the barred rock rooster, Rocky and the hens). A month or two ago, he decided Rocky could not come down to eat or be anywhere near his ladies. Our family went to bat for this lone guy and made sure he was taken care of while our hearts were hurting over the unfairness of it all. Well, something happened last week. Rocky had enough. He had been pressed over time. Courage rose from within him and showed our other rooster he was going to eat, mingle with the ladies, and go wherever he pleased.

Precious qualities are exposed when pressed. When grapes are pressed, wine is birthed. When olives are pressed, oil is driven out.

When put through fire, precious metals are purified. When people are pressed, character is refined. Through the process of pressing new and better qualities emerge. When Rocky the rooster suffered for a little while, courage appeared. This journey of life is complicated and not all roses. I have never met someone who had a perfect life. Sure, I have met plenty of people whose lives look perfect from the outside, but I bet if I took a closer look, I would be able to see hardship and painful experiences hidden underneath. I have learned that what matters is what we do when we are pressed. We get to choose. We can lash out on others, complain about the unfairness of it all, become the judge and jury, self-medicate, hide or fill our lives with so much *stuff* that we don't have time to deal with our pain, or we can press in and uncover our pearl from deep within.

Pretty imperfectly, I choose to press in. I press in to uncover the truest beauty. I press in to uncover the lies. I press in to untangle the mess. I press into truth. My pressing consists of talking to You, wrestling with You, sitting still in Your presence, reading Your word, crying, writing, singing, hanging out with other Christ followers, and taking one step at a time moving forward. As I press in, new life emerges. A newer version of the old me. A stronger me. A humbler me. A me with courage. A me set free from following the crowd. A more loving me. A more serving me. A refined me. Pressing in to find the real You in me. Not the me that is covered by the lies of this world, but the me that was designed and created for purpose. I have always been a little feisty. Feisty without You, Jesus, can be reckless, but feisty with purpose? Watch out world! I was designed to make a difference. I will press in for the win "and the God of all grace, who called you to his eternal glory in Christ, after you have suffered a little while, will himself restore you and make you strong, firm and steadfast" (1 Pet. 5:10).

"See, I have refined you, though not as silver; I have tested you in the furnace of affliction" (Isa. 48:10).

SIXTY-FOUR

May 8, 2019
Dear Jesus,

> Which of you, if your son asks for bread, will give him a stone?
> Or if he asks for a fish, will give him a snake? If you, then, though
> you are evil, know how to give good gifts to your children, how
> much more will your Father in heaven give good gifts to those
> who ask him!
>
> Matthew 7:9–11

I am working through the book, *The Shelter of God's Promises,*
by Sheila Walsh. In chapter nine, day five, this verse is written. I then
read the words, "Jesus was saying, would a father trick his hungry son
and give him a stone instead of bread? Would he torment his son by
giving him a fish but one he can't eat?"

Jesus, can I just scream right now?! I do not like this verse one
bit. I began reading it. Re-reading it. And still. Still, I do not like
it. I underline the two questions with dark uneven lines and then I
scribbled on the side of my book, "What about me, God? Is this true
for me?" The word *father* just stares at me. It is like the flashing neon
light hanging above the neighborhood saloon. A beacon of light.
Glaring at me. Begging me to look; come close. And I do what I
always do, wrestle with You. How does this affect me? Is this true for
me? How can this be true for me? This does not seem fair!

I have deep wounds caused by one of my parents. I have deep
scars; maybe visible, maybe invisible. Sometimes I feel like I got the
short end of the stick. Dealt a bad hand. I have been tricked and lied
to by a parent. I have been tormented by the hand of a parent. How

do I swallow these words from Matthew 7?

I began to dive into the text. Scouring for clarity. Trying to make sense of this verse that cuts me to the core. Earthly parents are sinners just like us (Rom. 3:23). No one is perfect, not even one (Rom. 3:10). It states that if our earthly parents who are evil, know how to give good gifts to Your children, how much more will your Father in heaven give good gifts to those who ask him. It does state, though you are evil. And it does state, how much more will your heavenly Father give. I cling to those two words. Evil and more. Sinners and God. Evil and holy. This is the truth. We can offer nothing to a holy God (Isa. 64:6) and He always does immeasurably more than we ask or imagine (Eph. 3:20). The screaming in my head begins to settle to a low roar. As I continue to mull it over and ask You to continue showing me truth, a question appeared in my mind, was it all bad?

This question startled me. The floodgate opened, and ugly tears spilled onto the steering wheel. Forgiveness is hard. Really hard, but necessary to move forward in freedom. You forgive me daily and so I too forgive those who have hurt me. (Matt. 6:14–15) So, I allow the process. The ugly, beautiful process of exposing pain so I can be healed. My mind drifts over my life. I begin to visualize myself walking through water. There is resistance and I begin to use my arms to pull through the current. I begin wading through the mess while keeping my eyes on things above (Col. 3:2). The gifts I swam to find today are these: my dad made sure he was a part of my life. He took me fishing and hiking in the Boone Ledges. We had the best Frosty fights and he always brought Life Savers to church and Hot Tamales in the car. He took me for Starbucks ice cream in the summer. When everyone got a new pogo-ball, he took me to the mall and bought me one and then drove me to the park so I could try it out. He never raised his voice and he never physically hurt me. He always told me he loved me. He called me smart and beautiful. For these gifts, I am eternally grateful.

This life is challenging, but so much more worth it when we dig to find the buried treasure. Jesus, You were falsely accused, arrested, denied, betrayed, mocked and beaten (Matt. 26 and 27) and You said, "Father, forgive them, for they do not know what they are doing (Luke 23:34). Even at death You, Jesus, were *love* (John 4:8). All I know is You care about me (1 Pet. 5:7). You do not want religion. You want me. A relationship with me. As I walk with You through this life, I will let You teach me how to forgive and love so I can be free.

SIXTY-FIVE

May 14, 2019
Dear Jesus,

Perfection is overrated. Be you. Be authentic. Be flawed. We are all one word away from slipping up. We are all one choice away from making a fool of ourselves. We are all one action away from losing credibility.

I hold myself to a high standard. I want to be perfect. Long to be righteous. Desire a flawless life. I am a gospel girl who loves You, Jesus. I love sharing Your word and telling all the wonderful things You have done. As a steward of Yours, I would never want to say or do anything that would misrepresent You and Your word. There is an issue with my high standard though. I can never live up to it. I will sometimes mis-speak. I will sometimes make poor choices. I may even do something that will affect my credibility. It may even happen in the presence of witnesses. You know how I know this? I am a daughter, a sister, a wife, a mother and a friend and I mess up. It has been proven time and time again. You know what the beautiful part of a life with You is?

There is now no condemnation for those who are in Christ Jesus, because through Christ Jesus the law of the Spirit who gives life has set you free from the law of sin and death. For what the law was powerless to do because it was weakened by the flesh, God did by sending his own Son in the likeness of sinful flesh to be a sin offering.

Romans 8:1–3

It is because of You that I am in Christ Jesus, who has become for me wisdom from God—that is, my righteousness, holiness, and redemption (1 Cor. 1:30). Because You died in my place, I am covered by Your blood which makes me perfect, righteous, and flawless. I could never do this on my own. I was never meant to. You are my righteousness.

As a Christian woman I long to be the perfect Proverbs 31 mother.

A wife of noble character who can find? She is worth far more than rubies. Her husband has full confidence in her and lacks nothing of value. She brings him good, not harm, all the days of her life. She selects wool and flax and works with eager hands. She is like the merchant ships, bringing her food from afar. She gets up while it is still night; she provides food for her family and portions for her female servants. She considers a field and buys it; out of her earnings she plants a vineyard. She sets about her work vigorously; her arms are strong for her tasks She sees that her trading is profitable, and her lamp does not go out at night. In her hand she holds the distaff and grasps the spindle with her fingers. She opens her arms to the poor and extends her hands to the needy. When it snows, she has no fear for her household; for all of them are clothed in scarlet. She makes coverings for her bed; she is clothed in fine linen and purple.

Her husband is respected at the city gate, where he takes his seat among the elders of the land. She makes linen garments and sells them, and supplies the merchants with sashes. She is clothed with strength and dignity; she can laugh at the days to come. She speaks with wisdom, and faithful instruction is on her tongue. She watches over the affairs of her household and does not eat the bread of idleness. Her children arise and call her blessed; her husband also, and he praises her: "Many women do noble things, but you surpass them all." Charm is deceptive, and beauty is fleeting; but a woman who fears the LORD is to be praised. Honor her for all that her hands have done, and let her works bring her praise at the city gate.

Proverbs 31:10–31

As I read the "Epilogue: The Wife of Noble Character," I find many attributes I long to possess. She is hard-working and wise. She is generous, kind, and compassionate. The Proverbs 31 girl is strong and faithful. Her husband and children rise and call her blessed. However, as I read and re-read the epilogue, I noticed something. She was not noted for all the things she did and all her wonderful character traits. She was noted for one thing and one thing only. "Many women do noble things, but you surpass them all." Charm is deceptive, and beauty is fleeting; but a woman who fears the LORD is to be praised. (Prov. 31:29–30) I believe this is the key to everything. Her fear of the LORD is what makes her beautiful and praiseworthy.

I want to be this. A woman who fears the LORD. Not in a shameful, never good enough, works based way, but in an awe and wonder, praise the LORD for what He has done, way. I will keep this in perspective. You are God and I am not. I could never measure up to who You are and what You have done. You are holy and I am not. "For it is by grace you have been saved, through faith—and this is not from yourselves, it is the gift of God— not by works, so that no one can boast" (Eph. 2:8–9). I will choose to be me, be authentic, be flawed, and I will mess up and take my humble place and ask for forgiveness. I will then pick myself back up, dust off my pants, and get moving. Perfection is overrated.

SIXTY-SIX

June 11, 2019
Dear Jesus,

I am my biggest obstacle. You know this. You must rid me of me. What if my biggest trial is my best gift? A gift that births lasting life. Not just getting by, complacency, but life in the fullest. A life free of myself, my mind, my thought patterns, my past, and my hurts.

In 2007, we were in a predicament. My family was scrambling to free ourselves of our challenge and made a choice. We bought an additional piece of property we intended to build on and one day move to. Life continued, time went on, and everything we thought we wanted was held from us. We remained in a home and holding pattern we could not escape. As time lapsed, we found ourselves in a community we loved. Time grew us and changed us and our desires. Our desire to move to this location dissipated and we continued life. We cared for the property; mowing, shoveling, and paying taxes. Holding on. Just holding on. What if? What if we still want it? What if we need it some day? What if? What if? What if? Sometimes it is just time to let go. Trust and move forward. We decided to build a house on our lot and sell the property.

Yesterday was D-day! (Dig Day) It was exciting! The piece of property began changing before my very eyes. I was mesmerized by the large machinery and the ease to which it removed the soil. Soil that had been untouched for years. Cars stopped, people stopped, all watching the land that had been vacant for so many years transform into something new. As the machine was peeling up the earth, I was thinking maybe this is what You do to us. You peel off any layer that is unfruitful. Over the last few years, I feel like I have been having a daily peel. Buh-bye pride. See you later fear. Do not come back envy, strife, unforgiveness, and hate. We must peel back the earth to make room for the new house. You must peel off the dead skin so I too can have a new house. A house that has room for love, joy, peace, patience, kindness, goodness. You transform me into something new. Something that looks a little more like You.

Over the last sixteen years, I have changed. Transformed. Not by choice, but by circumstance. Your circumstance. You mold those who love You and seek You. You have plans and a purpose for those who follow You. Marriage is challenging and requires selflessness. Raising children is challenging and requires selflessness. Being a neighbor is challenging and requires selflessness. Being a friend is challenging and requires selflessness. Being a Christ-follower is challenging and requires selflessness. The only way to become selfless is to be stripped. Completely stripped. Stripped of comfort, predictability, and control. What if You holding me in this place for too long, allowing suffering to occur, constant challenges and deep loss all were gifts of Your great mercy? These lessons catapulted me to new life. A life of truth and wholeness I never knew existed.

In this place is where I met You, Jesus, intimately. It was where I learned You are always near. You hear me and love me. It is where I learned You have a plan and a purpose for me. It is where I began to see the Spirit move. Where the Bible once was gibberish now was alive leaping off these pages. Where everything was so wrong the only thing that could be right was the truth littered through the pages. Where I learned to praise You in the storm. Where I kneeled in private. Cried in private. Prayed through my days. Worshipped in song. Where You gifted me with sweet whispers. Painted me pictures in the sky and revealed answers to secret requests. Where desires emerged from a new heart. Where I learned only You, Jesus, satisfies. Where a tenacious girl was made. Where strength blossomed and a voice was made.

This process of restoration was not fun, and I do not want to do one ounce of it over. However, the joy mingled with the pain was magical. How could there be so much pain yet so much joy at the same time? I do not know. A life with You and the Spirit is mesmerizing. You allowed me to go to places I could have never gone on my own. When my only possible answer is You, Jesus, and I see You come through?! Awe and wonder. Plain and simple. I know I am not finished or complete. I am a work in progress, but I have come a long way, baby! I will press on toward the goal. A life of joy, love, and peace.

As You continue to mold and shape me into Your likeness, I am beginning to see I play a role in this. I can just believe You are the God of miracles or I can believe You are the God of miracles and I can participate. I am learning to participate. Move over self and make room because this girl is going to: Practice what I preach. Be involved in my journey to wholeness. Surrender. Sacrifice. Obey. Love. Serve. Share. Step up. Step out. Be fearless. And unstoppable.

SIXTY-SEVEN

July 10, 2020
Dear Jesus,

Excitement bubbled up within me as I prepared to share my manuscript with an acquisition's editor. The visit was short and once again the excitement evaporated quickly; however, clarity came in and enveloped me in a garment of peace. The world was telling me to climb a platform ladder to the top and my spirit was telling me stay low, be humble, and serve. Your Holy Spirit was whispering truth I desperately needed to hear. Not by might, nor by power, but by my Spirit (Zech. 13:9). I will do immeasurably more than you ask or imagine (Eph. 3:20). I will supply all your needs and complete the work I began in you (Phil. 4:19). In one moment, I knew the truth. You planted this story in me and if You want it to go out to Your people, it will.

I came home from the conference with a new approach. I laid everything I have been working so hard on including my hopes and dreams at Your feet. I embarked on a new ministry opportunity to serve at church and I began once again following Your lead. I continued being a student of Your word and began taking classes to become a better steward and servant for Your kingdom. My focus has changed, Jesus. My only desire is to pursue You and watch You reign, equip me, and fulfill the plans You have for me.

CONCLUSION

July 10, 2020

This is the story of my redemptive walk with Jesus. This has been my personal journey in finding healing, wholeness, and purpose. Jesus set me free from self, control, insecurity, people-pleasing, and fear. He taught me about the abundant life He offers through His son. By His authority I have learned to speak life and truth into my own life, my marriage, my children, my home, and my circumstances. I have found Jesus offers a life free of division, chaos, and doubt. In Him, we have a life full of love, joy, peace, patience, kindness, goodness, faithfulness, gentleness, and self-control. Our God is the God of redemption. Beautiful redemption. "And we know that in all things God works for the good of those who love him, who have been called according to his purpose" (Rom. 8:28).

EPILOGUE

Dear Jesus is not a book about all the answers. It is about a Father who imparts wisdom to His child by the power of the Holy Spirit. Kari heard her Father's voice and in obedience and faith stepped out. She believed without seeing. Kari responded despite her fear, feelings, thoughts, and weaknesses. She decided to trust her Father's words.

"I will repay you for the years the locusts have eaten" (Joel 2:25).

"And who knows but that you have come to your royal position for such a time as this" (Esth. 4:14).

Kari realized her Father was bigger than anything she had ever done and anything that had ever happened to her. She decided to go ahead and receive everything her father said was hers. She decided she would not quit until she saw His words revealed in her life. Kari decided to take her eyes off what she could see and believe she could do anything she decided to do. Nothing was impossible for her (Luke 1:37). She knew He would do immeasurably more than she asked or imagined (Eph.3:20). She knew, "What no eye has seen, what no ear has heard, and what no human mind has conceived the things her father had planned for her" (1 Cor. 2:9).

NOTES

Chapter 6
1. Leave it to Beaver. Joe Connelly, Bob Mosher. CBS, October 1957.
2. Rocky. John G. Avildsen. Chartoff-Winkler Productions, 1976.
3. "Jesus Loves Me" (Warner, 1859)

Chapter 12
1. "10,000 Reasons" (Redman, Angrisano, 2013)

Chapter 13
1. "While I'm Waiting" (Waller, 2007)
2. Fireproof. Alex Kendrick. Albany: Sherwood Pictures, 2008.

Chapter 14
1. "In Christ Alone" (Townend, Getty, 2001)

Chapter 15
1. "King of My Heart" (McMillan, CCLI 7046145)

Chapter 59
1. "In Christ Alone" (Townend, Getty, 2001)

Chapter 61
1. Sheila Walsh, The Shelter of God's Promises: (Nashville, Thomas Nelson, 2011) 205.

Chapter 64
1. Sheila Walsh, The Shelter of God's Promises: (Nashville, Thomas Nelson, 2011) 205.

ABOUT THE AUTHOR

Kari Orloff is the owner of Beautiful Redemption, LLC and is a certified Christian Life Coach living in rural Blanchardville, Wisconsin. Kari is a Jesus-loving wife and mother and is a truth-seeker. Kari finds her truest joy and peace in writing about God's Word. She has personally experienced God's restoration power and longs to share the Good News. Kari desires to encourage others to arise and step into the purpose God planned in advance for them to walk.